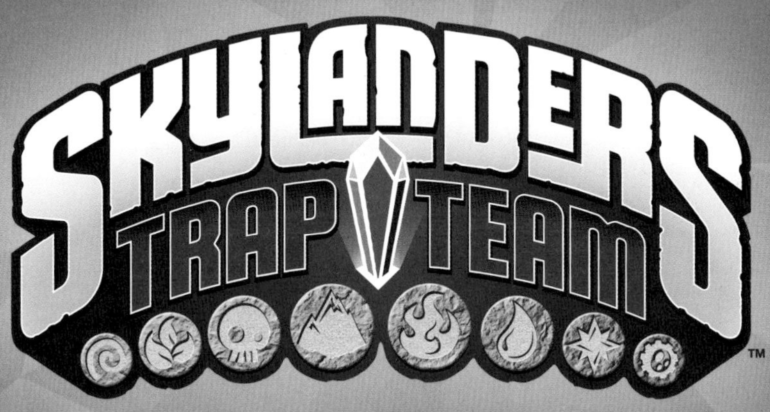

MASTER EON'S

OFFICIAL GUIDE

GROSSET & DUNLAP
Penguin Young Readers Group
An Imprint of Penguin Random House LLC

ISBN 978-0-448-48717-5 10 9 8 7 6 5 4 3 2 1

MASTER EON'S OFFICIAL GUIDE

Grosset & Dunlap
An Imprint of Penguin Random House

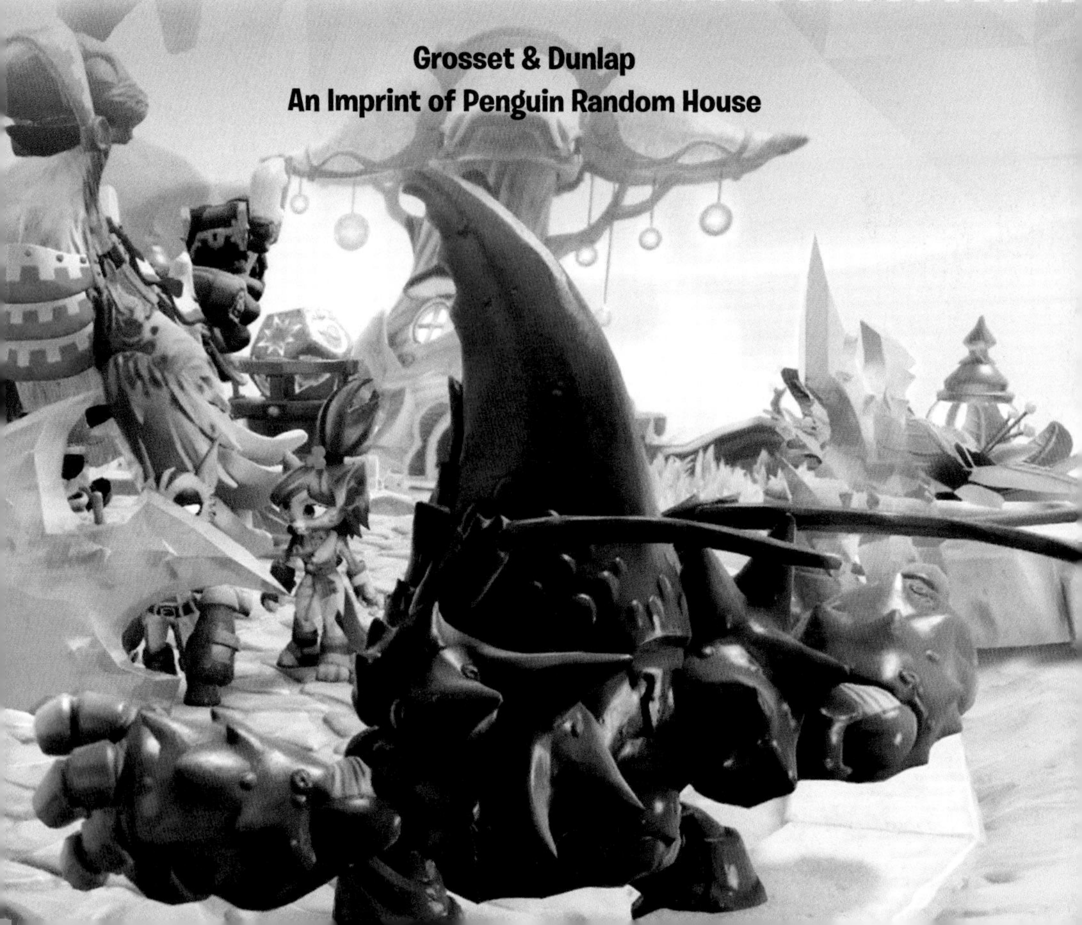

CONTENTS

WELCOME TO SKYLANDS

REIGN OF THE DOOM RAIDERS

Greetings, Portal Master. I am Eon, your guide throughout your latest adventure in Skylands. As you know, Skylands is a magical place, full of wonder and excitement and protected by those most heroic of heroes—the Skylanders.

The Doom Raiders

Long ago, it was a different case. The infinite islands of Skylands were blighted by a band of ruthless super criminals known as the Doom Raiders. They swarmed from the Savage Badlands to strike terror throughout Skylands, stealing anything that wasn't nailed down (and quite a few things that were, as well)!

Meet the Doom Raiders on page 109.

The Trap Masters

Hearing the cries of the Doom Raiders' victims, I sent in a crack team of Skylanders, each wielding elemental weapons of extreme power. This was the Trap Team!

The battle was fierce, but the Trap Masters were victorious. The Doom Raiders fell one by one, but I was all too aware that their evil must never be allowed to rise again.

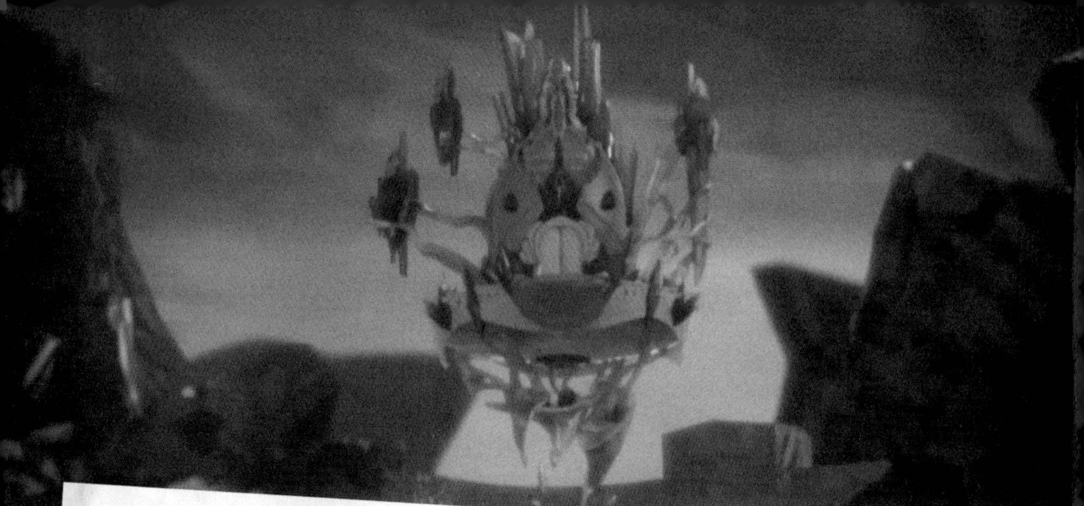

Cloudcracker Prison

To hold the Doom Raiders, the Skylanders constructed an impenetrable and inescapable fortress of pure **Traptanium**, one of the toughest materials in the known universe (and probably in the unknown universe to boot). Its name—Cloudcracker Prison!

The Doom Raiders were sealed within its **Traptanium** walls, guarded by the Trap Team day and—especially—night. Over time, other vile villains were sent to Cloudcracker, and peace returned to Skylands once more.

Until now!

Prison Break

Kaos, the most evil Portal Master in the history of, well, everything, has destroyed Cloudcracker Prison and banished the Trap Team to your planet.

You must find them, Portal Master, and the Elemental Traps created from the debris of the prison. Together, you and the Trap Team can capture the escaped Cloudcracker convicts. Once trapped, the Villains will switch sides, fighting alongside your Skylanders to defeat Kaos and his fiendish allies.

The future of Skylands is in your hands . . . again!

GETTING STARTED

SKYLANDER STATS

Your Skylanders may look like toys, but place them on your *Portal of Power* and they will return to Skylands to once again fight the forces of Darkness.

As you guide them through their adventures, your Skylanders will develop new abilities, becoming more and more powerful. Evildoers everywhere, beware!

You can check how your Skylanders are progressing by placing them on your *Traptanium Portal*. What are you waiting for? Try one now.

STAT-PACK! Here is what those Skylander Stats mean!

Maximum Health	How much damage can your Skylander withstand in battle? This much!
Armor	How strong are their defenses?
Speed	Just how fast can they move?
Critical Hit	How much damage can they dish out?

***EON'S** TIP*

See the Elemental Power Stat? The more Skylanders you collect in each Element, the more their power grows!

What's in a name?

Always thought Shroomboom should have been called Onk? Well, you can change the name of any Skylander by going to the NICKNAME control.

But, seriously—Onk? Fine for a literary penguin, but a Skylander?

ELEMENTS

We always believed that the power that runs through Skylands was split into eight Elements. Each single Skylander is linked to a single Element, able to tap into its energy.

The Eight Elements are:

Air

Life

Fire

Magic

Earth

Undead

Water

Tech

Throughout Skylands, you'll discover that certain areas are also linked to a specific Element. For example, if an area favors the Water Element, try to use a Water Skylander. They'll receive more points when defeating enemies.

You'll also see special *Traptanium* Elemental Gates that can unlock special areas. Only Trap Masters of the Element shown on the gates can open them.

DARK AND LIGHT

The same colossal explosion that destroyed Cloudcracker Prison also fractured the very foundation of Skylands, exposing two new Elements:

Dark

Light

Who knows how many more Elements are out there? Flynn is hoping for an Enchilada Element, but I fear he will be disappointed!

THE NEXT LEVEL

LEVEL UP!

There are many ways to help your Skylander get stronger. First are the little experience orbs you'll see when you defeat an enemy. Absorb those to level up! Your Skylanders' health points will increase, meaning that they'll last longer in battle!

UPGRADES

Each and every Skylander starts their adventures with two spectacular powers, but that is only the beginning of their potential. Collect coins and treasure to purchase magical upgrades from Persephone the Fairy. You'll find her at Skylanders Academy or popping up from time to time on your missions.

PORTAL MASTER RANKS

It's not just Skylanders who can level up! As you guide your Skylanders forward, taking on more and more missions and completing more and more goals, you will be rewarded by ranking up at the end of every chapter. The more stars you get, the higher you'll rise! One day you may even be as powerful as I am!

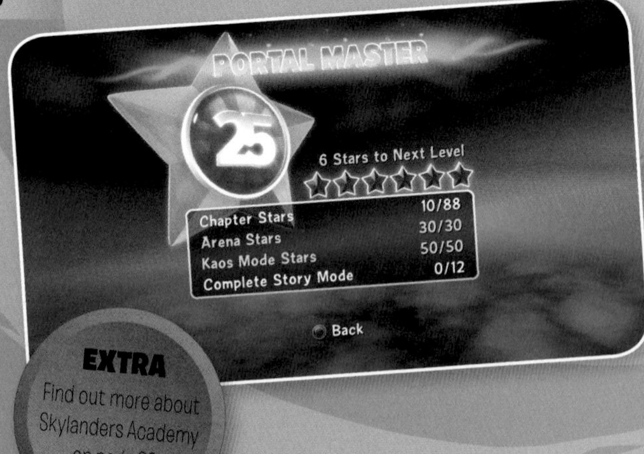

EXTRA

Find out more about Skylanders Academy on page 26.

COLLECTIBLE ITEMS

It's always good to keep your eyes peeled as you explore Skylands. Each island is dotted with collectible items that can help your Skylander succeed!

FOOD

Tasty treats can be found everywhere, and what good luck! These mighty morsels help boost your Skylanders' health after battle. Personally, I'm partial to cheese and sheep-wool pizza—or I was, when I still had a body!

TREASURE CHESTS

Long ago the legendary Sky Pirates hid treasure chests all over Skylands. Fortunately for you, the pirates were as forgetful as they were fearsome. Give every chest you find a quick shake. The booty within will help buy upgrades!

VILLAIN STASHES

Back in their horrendous heyday, the Doom Raiders hid their ill-gotten gains in vaults that can only be opened by Villains. Once you've got them trapped, use your converted Villains to unlock the contents inside!

WINGED SAPPHIRES

Some of the most elusive creatures in Skylands, these winged beauties are Persephone's favorite treasures. Collect them for her and she'll give you upgrade discounts.

SOUL GEMS

No one knows who scattered these valuable Gems across Skylands. Perhaps it was me on one of my more playful days? I forget. But find them and you'll unlock the ability to purchase even more powerful upgrades for your Skylanders.

STORY SCROLLS

Since we last met, Flynn has been writing his autobiography. Sadly, Skylands' number one pilot lost the scrolls in a scrape with a particularly windy Air Golem. His chapters have been blown across the islands. Can you find them all?

LEGENDARY TREASURES

As you'll discover in a few pages, a new Skylanders Academy is being built. You can help with the final decorations by discovering the Legendary Treasures stashed away on the islands you visit.

LEGENDARY TREASURE	LOCATION
Legendary Bubble Fish	Rainfish Riviera
Legendary Chompy Statue	Chompy Mountain
Legendary Clock	Time Town
Legendary Cyclops Teddy Bear	Telescope Towers
Legendary Dragon Head	The Golden Desert
Legendary Eel Plunger	Secret Sewers of Supreme Stink
Legendary Egg	The Phoenix Psanctuary
Legendary Flynn Statue	Nightmare Express
Legendary Gargoyle	Midnight Museum
Legendary Geode Key	Skyhighlands
Legendary Golden Frog	Monster Marsh
Legendary Hippo Head	Lair of the Golden Queen
Legendary Knight Statue	Sunscraper Spire
Legendary Masterpieces	Wilikin Workshop
Legendary Parachuting Mabu	Operation: Troll Rocket Steal
Legendary Pepper Chest	Chef Zeppelin
Legendary Rocket	The Future of Skylands
Legendary Saw Blade	Mystic Mill
Legendary Statue	Know-It-All Island
Legendary Weird Robot	The Ultimate Weapon
Legendary Windmill	Mirror of Mystery

When you bring the Treasures back to the Academy, you'll unlock the finishing touches to the castle. I'm particularly fond of the Legendary Bubble Fish, myself. So calming, especially if you're a disembodied spirit. You've no idea how stressful it can get!

HATS

Don't ever laugh at a Skylander who is wearing a silly hat. Magical headgear is a great way to boost their powers. Seek out the hatboxes hidden away all around Skylands.

NAME	BONUS POINTS	LOCATION
Alarm Clock Hat	+10 Armor +4 Speed	Time Town
Batter Up Hat	+15 Critical Hit +12 Armor	The Golden Desert
Beetle Hat	+30 Armor	Lair of the Golden Queen
Bobby	+20 Armor +7 Elemental Power	Time Town
Brain Hat	+37 Elemental Power	The Ultimate Weapon
Brainiac Hat	+15 Critical Hit +6 Speed	The Ultimate Weapon
Bronze Arkeyan Helm	+25 Critical Hit +15 Armor +4 Speed	Skylanders Academy
Bucket Hat	+5 Armor	Soda Springs
Candle Hat	+25 Elemental Power	Rumble Club
Ceiling Fan Hat	+5 Critical Hit +5 Armor	The Phoenix Psanctuary
Classic Pot Hat	+30 Armor	Lair of the Golden Queen
Clown Bowler Hat	+20 Critical Hit	Wilikin Workshop
Clown Classic Hat	+20 Elemental Power	Monster Marsh
Colander Hat	+10 Armor	Chef Zeppelin
Core of Light Hat	+12 Critical Hit +8 Speed	Skylanders Academy
Crazy Light Bulb Hat	+12 Speed	Lair of the Golden Queen
Cubano Hat	+7 Speed +7 Elemental Power	Operation: Troll Rocket Steal
Daisy Crown	+5 Critical Hit +2 Speed	The Phoenix Psanctuary
Desert Crown	+27 Elemental Power	The Golden Desert
Dragon Skull	+5 Critical Hit +10 Armor	Monster Marsh

NAME	BONUS POINTS	LOCATION
Eggshell Hat	+25 Armor	Rumble Club
Extreme Viking Hat	+15 Critical Hit +10 Elemental Power	The Future of Skylands
Garrison Hat	+20 Armor	Mystic Mill
Gold Arkeyan Helm	+37 Critical Hit +20 Armor +8 Speed	Skylanders Academy
Hedgehog Hat	+2 Speed +2 Elemental Power	Know-It-All Island
Horns Be With You Hat	+7 Elemental Power	Chompy Mountain
Hunting Hat	+2 Critical Hit +2 Armor	Chompy Mountain
Imperial Hat	+7 Armor +2 Speed	Rainfish Riviera
Juicer Hat	+12 Armor +5 Speed	Chef Zeppelin
Kepi Hat	+25 Critical Hit +2 Speed	Operation: Troll Rocket Steal
Kokoshnik	+30 Elemental Power	The Future of Skylands
Lil' Elf Hat	+8 Speed	Wilikin Workshop
Melon Hat	+5 Elemental Power	Soda Springs
Metal Fin Hat	+12 Critical Hit	Rainfish Riviera
Monday Hat	+10 Critical Hit	Operation: Troll Rocket Steal
Mountie Hat	+15 Armor	Mystic Mill
Night Cap	+25 Critical Hit	Rumble Club
Nurse Hat	+30 Armor	Operation: Troll Rocket Steal
Old-Time Movie Hat	+15 Elemental Power	Telescope Towers
Paperboy Hat	+4 Speed	Chompy Mountain
Parrot Nest	+7 Speed	The Phoenix Psanctuary
Planet Hat	+10 Speed	Rumble Club
Pyramid Hat	+20 Critical Hit +10 Armor	Rumble Club

NAME	BONUS POINTS	LOCATION
Radar Hat	+5 Critical Hit +5 Armor	Skyhighlands
Raver Hat	+5 Armor +8 Speed	Skylanders Academy
Rubber Glove Hat	+12 Critical Hit +12 Armor	Secret Sewers of Supreme Stink
Rugby Hat	+7 Critical Hit +3 Speed	Telescope Towers
Scooter Hat	+10 Elemental Power	Chef Zeppelin
Shadow Ghost Hat	+20 Critical Hit +7 Armor	Monster Marsh
Shire Hat	+5 Armor +9 Speed	Skylanders Academy
Shower Cap	+6 Speed	Secret Sewers of Supreme Stink
Silver Arkeyan Helm	+30 Critical Hit +17 Armor +6 Speed	Skylanders Academy
Skipper Hat	+5 Armor	Know-It-All Island
Sleuth Hat	+7 Critical Hit	Know-It-All Island
Steampunk Hat	+17 Armor	Rainfish Riviera
Synchronized Swimming Hat	+10 Critical Hit +10 Armor	Telescope Towers
Tin Foil Hat	+10 Armor +15 Elemental Power	The Future of Skylands
Trash Lid	+10 Armor +10 Elemental Power	Secret Sewers of Supreme Stink
Turtle Hat	+7 Armor	Soda Springs
Volcano Hat	+15 Critical Hit	Mystic Mill
Weather Vane Hat	+25 Armor	Soda Springs
William Tell Hat	+25 Critical Hit	Skyhighlands
Wizard Hat	+10 Critical Hit +10 Speed	Rumble Club
Wooden Hat	+17 Critical Hit +5 Armor	Skylanders Academy

More hats can be purchased from Auric's store and Hatterson's Hat Shop at Skylanders Academy. Now, why isn't there an Eon Hat, hmmm?

TRINKETS

Trinkets are the latest fashion statement in Skylands. Find them throughout Skylanders Academy, buy them from Auric's shop, or earn them by reaching a new Portal Master rank. Your Skylanders—and captured Villains—will wear these trinkets with pride! I gave my assistant, Hugo, a sheep trinket last week. He still hasn't come out from under the bed!

TRINKET	HOW TO GET IT
Batterson's Bubble	Portal Master Rank 4
Big Bow of Boom	Skylanders Academy after Chapter 2
Billy Bison	Skylanders Academy
Blobbers's Medal of Courage	Auric's Shop after Chapter 4
Bubble Blower	Auric's Shop after Chapter 2
Cyclops's Spinner	Portal Master Rank 38
Dark Water Daisy	Portal Master Rank 20
Elemental Diamond	Skylanders Academy after Chapter 1
Elemental Opal	Auric's Shop after Chapter 9
Elemental Radiant	Portal Master Rank 33
Goo Factory Gear	Auric's Shop after Chapter 4
Iris's Iris	Skylanders Academy after Chapter 2
Kuckoo Kazoo	Portal Master Rank 31
Lizard Lilly	Auric's Shop after Chapter 2
Mabu's Medallion	Portal Master Rank 29
Medal of Gallantry	Auric's Shop after Chapter 4
Medal of Heroism	Auric's Shop after Chapter 2
Medal of Mettle	Auric's Shop after Chapter 9
Medal of Valiance	Auric's Shop after Chapter 13
Pirate Pinwheel	Auric's Shop after Chapter 13
Ramses's Dragon Horn	Portal Master Rank 16
Ramses's Rune	Portal Master Rank 12
Seadog Seashell	Portal Master Rank 23
Snuckles's Sunflower	Auric's Shop after Chapter 4
Spyro's Shield	Skylanders Academy after Chapter 13
Stealth Elf's Gift	Skylanders Academy in the Grand Library (Minis only)
T-Bone's Lucky Tie	Portal Master Rank 26
Teddy Cyclops	Portal Master Rank 7
Time Town Ticker	Portal Master Rank 35
Ullysses Uniclops	Auric's Shop after Chapter 9
Vote for Cyclops	Auric's Shop after Chapter 2
Wilikin Windmill	Skylanders Academy
Winged Medal of Bravery	Auric's Shop after Chapter 9

SKYSTONES SMASH

Skystones Smash is a new game that is spreading like wildfire across Skylands. No, not like Wildfire the Trap Master. It's a turn of phrase. Oh, never mind, here's how to play.

1 Collect cards every time you capture a Villain.

2 Each player starts the game with a number of hearts. The aim of the game is to reduce the health of your opponent to zero before they do the same to you!

3 Each stone has two stats:

HEALTH How many rounds your stone can survive.

ATTACK How much damage your stone will cause per round.

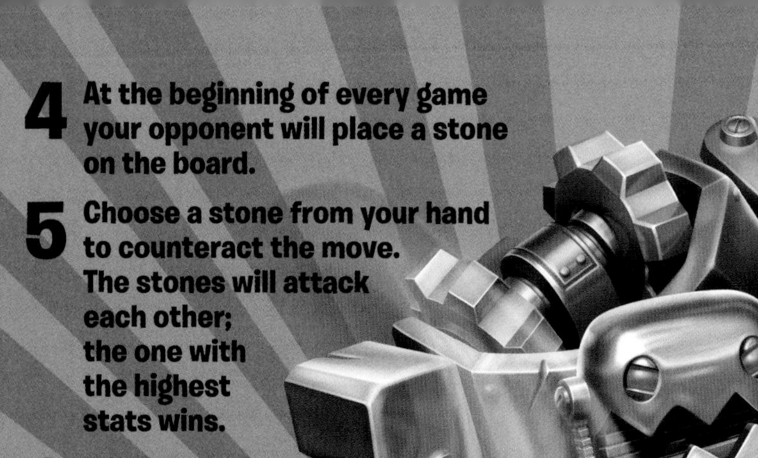

4 At the beginning of every game your opponent will place a stone on the board.

5 Choose a stone from your hand to counteract the move. The stones will attack each other; the one with the highest stats wins.

6 If no stone blocks yours, you will take at least one heart from your opponent.

7 Some stones have special powers, which can boost your game or weaken your opponent.

8 The first player to reduce their opponent to zero wins! Congratulations or commiserations, depending on how you've played!

Special Skystones Smash Stones

Fireball
Damage all enemy cards in play.

Lightning
Damage the other player.

Heartboost
Gain extra lives.

Sheepify
Turn an enemy card into a sheep.

WELCOME TO SKYLANDERS ACADEMY

MEET MAGS

The Academy is still being built, with new wings appearing after every level. Mags, the resident genius inventor, will be on hand to tell you what's new. She went to inventing school with Dr. Krankcase, you know. I know which pupil I prefer!

FLYNN THE PILOT

Flynn is always on hand to take you on a mission or tell you how great he is. Most of the time, it's both!

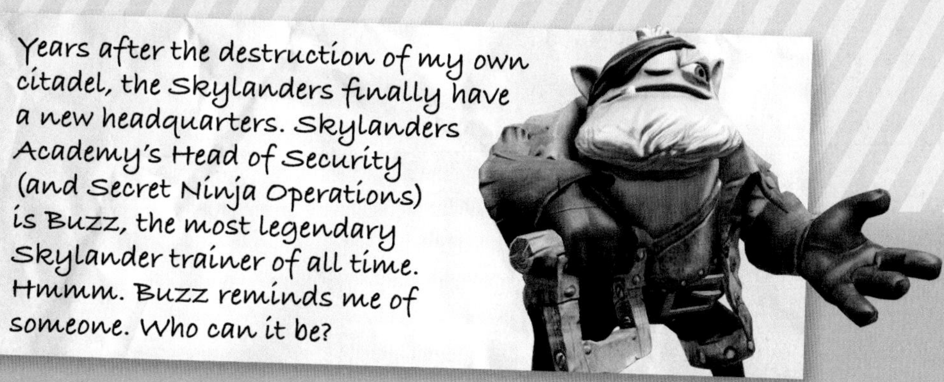

Years after the destruction of my own citadel, the Skylanders finally have a new headquarters. Skylanders Academy's Head of Security (and Secret Ninja Operations) is Buzz, the most legendary Skylander trainer of all time. Hmmm. Buzz reminds me of someone. Who can it be?

VILLAIN VAULT

Every Villain you trap will be stored in here, ready to be placed in a trap between missions!

KAOS DOOM CHALLENGE

Kaos has managed to curse the new Skylander training area. Head over to his statue to try your hand (or claw or piston or whatever you have) at his fiendish trials.

HINT

There are teleporters hidden around the Academy that zap you from one place to another. Now, where did they put the observatory teleporter?

MAIN HALL

Here you will find Auric's store. It's full of trinkets, hats, and other useful tools. Hmmm. What's that behind the fireplace?

EON'S TIP

Spot any jiggling cupboard doors? Smash them open to see what's inside.

PERSEPHONE'S TREE HOUSE

On your first visit, you may find a little trinket to brighten your day. You can also head back here to get upgrades from Persephone.

GAME ROOM

Need to practice Skystones Smash? Then head up to the Game Room in the Upper Hallway! Dreadbeard is always up for a game.

EXTRA

The Game Room stepping-stones can be operated only by a Skylander matching the Element on each of the slabs.

SKALETONES SHOWDOWN

Want to top the Skylands charts? Then take Crossbones's challenge and join the Skaletones. Can you keep the beat?

HINT

Hatterson's Hat Store is also on the Upper Hallway, although the marvelous milliner is being menaced by trolls. Can you help?

THE GRAND LIBRARY

Ah, Hugo's favorite place, found on the Outer Walkway. Quigley is training to be a Skylander and has already found his way into the secret Archives hidden behind a bookshelf. Can you find other secret levels around the Academy?

MEET THE TRAP MASTERS

MAGIC

BLASTERMIND

"MIND OVER MATTER!"

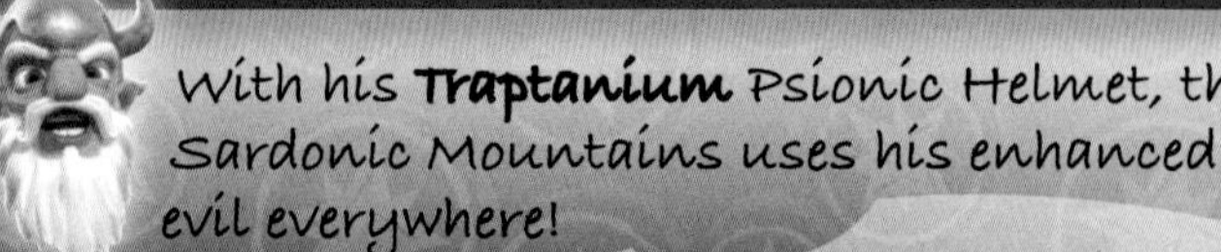

With his **Traptanium** Psionic Helmet, this native of the Sardonic Mountains uses his enhanced brainpower to fight evil everywhere!

SOUL GEM
in Skyhighlands

LOCK PUZZLE PSYCHIC Solve Lock Puzzles in an actual flash!

STARTING STATS	
Max Health	240
Armor	30
Speed	70
Critical Hit	50
Elemental Power	25

PERSONALITY FILE

- Calm
- Controlled
- Clever
- Persuasive

Starting Powers

Attack 1

BRAINWAVES Blast enemies with the power of your mighty mind!

Attack 2

LEVITATION Levitate your foes–and then bash them into the ground!

Power Upgrades

500 Gold

TASTY WAVES Brainwave attacks last longer!

700 Gold

BRAIN FREEZE Energy balls give enemies pause for thought!

900 Gold

BRAIN STORM Nothing will shelter your enemies from a psychic storm.

1,200 Gold

DOWN TO EARTH Levitated foes damage their evil allies when they come back to Earth.

"Choose Your Path" Upgrades

Path 1: Psychokinetic Raise the levitation stakes

1,700 Gold

BRAIN BLOWOUT Levitated enemies get blasted!

2,200 Gold

REMOTE CONTROL Foes you levitate become yours to command!

3,000 Gold

MIND MASH Levitation leads to multiple smash-downs!

Path 2: Mentalist Mind control matters!

1,700 Gold

MIND CONTROL Energy balls take control of minions' minds.

2,200 Gold

THE MORE THE MERRIER Levitate a bunch of bad guys at once!

3,000 Gold

MIND BLOWN Mind-controlled minions damage their bad-tempered buddies.

MAGIC

ENIGMA

"OUT OF SIGHT!"

Enigma cut himself off from his own magical realm to save his people from the Darkness. His sacrifice proved he was worthy of becoming a Trap Master.

SOUL GEM
in Operation: Troll Rocket Steal

AN EYE FOR SEVERAL EYES
A beam of brilliant light blasts from your staff's eye!

STARTING STATS

Max Health	310
Armor	30
Speed	60
Critical Hit	60
Elemental Power	25

PERSONALITY FILE

Mysterious
Otherworldly
Protective
Brave

Starting Powers

Attack 1

MYSTIC STAFF Minions mystically mashed!

Attack 2

INVISIBILITY MODE It's easy to see why this is useful! Or, rather, it isn't.

Power Upgrades

500 Gold

PARADOX POUND A staff slam that causes strife to all nearby foes.

900 Gold

CLOAK AND DAGGER Your cloak becomes a weapon as invisibility lasts longer.

700 Gold

MAGIC MIST Cover your enemies in a menacing mist!

1,200 Gold

PARADOX POWER Your Paradox Pound gets a power-up!

"Choose Your Path" Upgrades

Path 1: Chief of Staff Soup up your Mystic Staff

1,700 Gold

EYE SLAM COMBO Super-slam your Mystic Staff.

2,200 Gold

CLOAK DASH COMBO Your enemies will never see you coming!

3,000 Gold

IT'S RAINING EYES? Magic eyes drop from the skies!

Path 2: Invisible Invader Super see-through skills!

1,700 Gold

NINJA STYLE Invisible attacks are more intense!

2,200 Gold

MIND-BOGGLING Paradox Pound knocks enemies back.

3,000 Gold

GIVE UP THE GHOST Ghostly doppelgängers appear in Invisibility Mode.

WATER

SNAP SHOT

"CROC AND ROLL!"

After wiping out every Chompy in his Swamplands home, this fearless Crocagator became Skylands' greatest monster hunter. Is it any wonder that I asked him to hunt our most dangerous Villains?

SOUL GEM
in The Phoenix Psanctuary

A SHARD ACT TO FOLLOW
Perform a Crystal Slam in midair.

STARTING STATS

Max Health	290
Armor	24
Speed	70
Critical Hit	30
Elemental Power	25

PERSONALITY FILE

- Persistent
- Thorough
- Determined
- Focused

Starting Powers

Attack 1

***TRAPTANIUM* ARROWS** Make sure enemies get the point!

Attack 2

CRYSTAL SLAM Slam your *Traptanium* sword!

Power Upgrades

500 Gold

SURE SHOT CROC Charge up your bow and *Traptanium* arrows!

900 Gold

SUPER SLAM Your Crystal Slam just got stronger!

700 Gold

TORRENTIAL TIDEPOOL Wash away wicked enemies.

1,200 Gold

AMAZING ARROW New arrowhead, new danger!

"Choose Your Path" Upgrades

Path 1: Crack Shot Croc Top *Traptanium* Arrow Armory

1,700 Gold

ARROWSPLOSION Your arrowheads now go boom on impact!

2,200 Gold

***TRAPTANIUM* FLECHETTE** Shards of *Traptanium* shoot from your arrows.

3,000 Gold

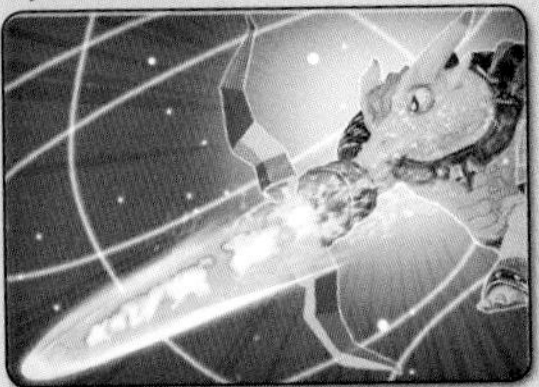

HYDRO ARROW Arrows make a bigger splash.

Path 2: Tide Turner Tune up your Tidal Attacks

1,700 Gold

BIG WAVE TORRENT Torrents become more torrential!

2,200 Gold

WATER TRAP Enemies trapped in torrents can't get out. Glub!

3,000 Gold

WHAT'S KRAKEN? Your torrents get their own sea monsters! How cute!

WATER

LOB-STAR

"STAR BRIGHT, STAR FIGHT!"

Once an underwater chef, crustacean crusader Lob-Star swam into action when an over-large Leviathan tried to swallow the King of the Fishes.

SOUL GEM
in Rainfish Riviera

HARD BOILED Send out a storm of super steam.

STARTING STATS	
Max Health	240
Armor	30
Speed	60
Critical Hit	40
Elemental Power	25

PERSONALITY FILE

Secretive
Risk-taker
Steamed
Berserker

Starting Powers

Attack 1

STARSHOOTER Fling *Traptanium* Flying Stars.

Attack 2

BOILING TEMPER Get steamed up to increase your strength!

Power Upgrades

500 Gold

LOB-STAR ROLL Barge into battle.

900 Gold

BOILING OVER Let off more steam!

700 Gold

SHARP SHOT Even sharper shooting stars.

1,200 Gold

LOB-STAR EXPRESS Your Lob-Star Roll repels wrongdoers!

"Choose Your Path" Upgrades

Path 1: Shooting Star Throwing skills tune-up!

1,700 Gold

SUPER STARS When boiled, *Traptanium* Stars slice through enemies.

2,200 Gold

TWICE THE STARPOWER Lob two *Traptanium* Stars at once!

3,000 Gold

STAR DEFENSE Send even more stars flying.

Path 2: The Boiler Control your temper!

1,700 Gold

GETTING STEAMED! Automatically blast steam at baddies when hit.

2,200 Gold

SELF E-STEAM Get super steamy with less boiling required!

3,000 Gold

FULL STEAM AHEAD Leave a scorching, steamy trail.

FIRE WILDFIRE

"BRINGING THE HEAT!"

Shunned by his fellow lions because he is made of solid gold, Wildfire proved his precious mettle when he saved the Fire Claw Clan from a flaming scorpion.

SOUL GEM
in Telescope Towers

LION FORM Become the King of the Blazing Beasts.

STARTING STATS	
Max Health	330
Armor	30
Speed	60
Critical Hit	30
Elemental Power	25

PERSONALITY FILE
- Brave-hearted
- Watchful
- Fierce
- Strong-willed

Starting Powers

Attack 1

***TRAPTANIUM* SHIELD BASH** When offense is the best defense!

Attack 2

CHAINS OF FIRE Burning chains drag enemies in.

Power Upgrades

500 Gold

HEAT SHIELD Protect yourself while damaging attackers.

900 Gold

FIRE ROAR Let enemies feel the warmth of your breath.

700 Gold

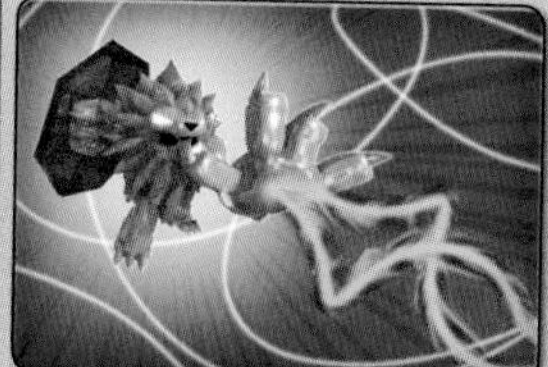

EXTRA CHAINS Pull in four enemies at once.

1,200 Gold

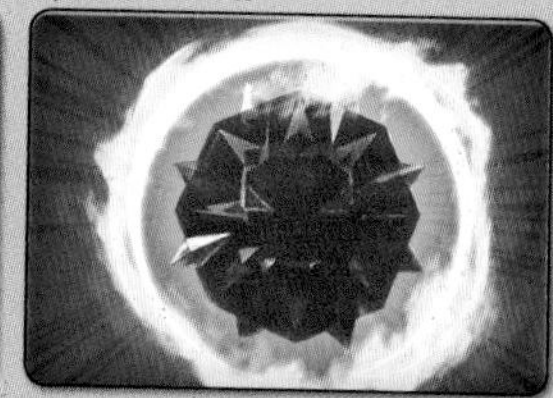

HOTTER HEAT SHIELD Flaming shield burns hotter than ever.

"Choose Your Path" Upgrades

Path 1: Shield Slasher Brilliant Shield Bashing!

1,700 Gold

BURNING BASH Heat up your Shield Bash.

2,200 Gold

FIRE SPIN Twist into a ring of fire!

3,000 Gold

SEARING SLAM Shield Bashes go supernova!

Path 2: Chain Champion Leave your enemies rattled!

1,700 Gold

LOTS OF CHAINS Link up with five enemies at once.

2,200 Gold

BLAZING BREATH Extend the range of your roar.

3,000 Gold

NO ESCAPE! Golden chain attacks reach farther.

FIRE KA-BOOM

"BOOM TIME!"

With the fabled Munitions Forge under attack from pirates, Ka-Boom constructed the fearsome Boom Cannon. The plundering Sky Pirates' hearts sank—and so did their ships!

SOUL GEM in The Ultimate Weapon

MISSILE RAIN Mortal Strikes burning brightly!

STARTING STATS	
Max Health	250
Armor	12
Speed	60
Critical Hit	80
Elemental Power	25

PERSONALITY FILE

- Inventive
- Hardworking
- Resourceful
- Constructive

Starting Powers

Attack 1

***TRAPTANIUM* CANNONBALLS** Ready! Aim! BOOM!

Attack 2

CANNON JUMP Blast yourself into the air.

Power Upgrades

500 Gold

JUMPQUAKE Cannon Jumps rumble up a destructive earthquake.

900 Gold

THE LONG RANGER Mortar Strikes fly farther.

700 Gold

MORTAR STRIKE What's fired up must come down.

1,200 Gold

CANNON CHARGE *Traptanium* Cannonballs do more damage.

"Choose Your Path" Upgrades

Path 1: Cannonball Runner Supercharge your cannonballs

1,700 Gold

BOUNCING BALLS Send your cannonballs ricocheting off walls.

2,200 Gold

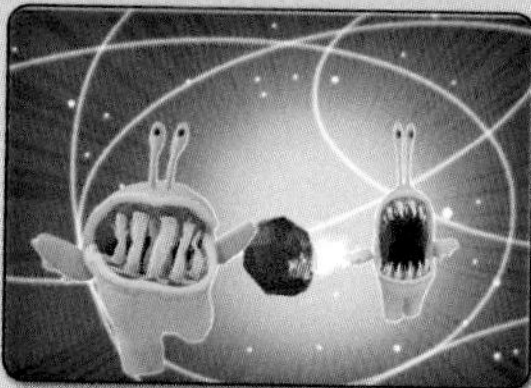

SUPER BOUNCING BALLS Cannonballs now bounce between bad guys.

3,000 Gold

TRIPLE SHOT Fire three cannonballs at once!

Path 2: Jumping Juggernaut Jump to it!

1,700 Gold

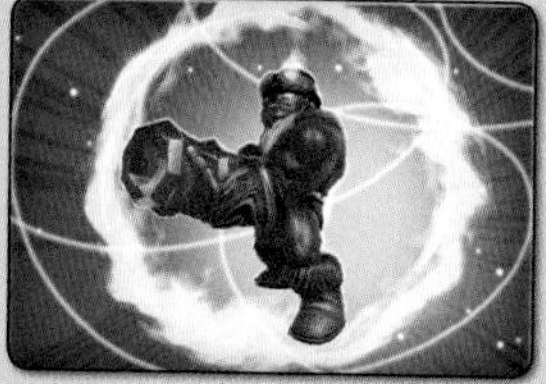

FIRE FLY Cannon Jumps flame-grill any foes in front of you.

2,200 Gold

BIG AIR Enemies are stunned by your giant leaps.

3,000 Gold

TRIPLE JUMP Three jumps in a row, no need to rest!

LIFE 

TUFF LUCK

"IT'S YOUR LUCKY DAY!"

Tuff Luck sprang into action when trolls tried to drain Fortunata Springs, the source of all good luck in Skylands. The trolls were ultimately unlucky, but I was fortunate enough to recruit Tuff Luck as a Trap Master.

SOUL GEM
in The Golden Desert

GARDEN OF PAIN The sharpest blades of grass you'll ever see.

STARTING STATS	
Max Health	310
Armor	48
Speed	85
Critical Hit	80
Elemental Power	25

PERSONALITY FILE

- Blessed with good luck
- Agile
- Quick-thinking
- Natural guardian

Starting Powers

Attack 1

TRAPTANIUM WARBLADES There's nothing lucky about feeling these bite.

Attack 2

POUNCE MODE Sneak up on your enemies and strike.

Power Upgrades

500 Gold

WARBLADE STAB Slice with your *Traptanium* Warblades.

900 Gold

CONTROL YOUR DESTINY Control exactly where the Warblade Stab strikes.

700 Gold

GREEN THUMB Pounce mode lasts longer.

1,200 Gold

GLAIVE WAVE Warblade attacks bring an energy blast.

"Choose Your Path" Upgrades

Path 1: Pouncy Pouncer Pep up your Pounce attacks

1,700 Gold

POISON IVY Pounce Mode leaves more poisonous clover patches.

2,200 Gold

POWERFUL POUNCE Pounce Mode has never been more powerful.

3,000 Gold

4-LEAF CLOVER Clover restores your health. Lucky for some!

Path 2: Warblade Whacker Become a Warblade wizard

1,700 Gold

WAVE GOOD-BYE Energy waves bring more bad fortune.

2,200 Gold

LUCKY SPIN Enjoy the sweet spin of success.

3,000 Gold

WINGIN' WARBLADE Weave a Warblade Windfall!

BUSHWHACK

"AXE TO THE MAX!"

Given an enchanted axe by Arbo the tree spirit, Bushwhack saved his tree-elf brothers from rampaging Lumberjack Trolls. The greenskins' tree-cutting machines were reduced to splinters, and Bushwhack joined the Trap Team.

SOUL GEM
in Chompy Mountain

TIMBER Grow a giant tree, then send it crashing down!

STARTING STATS

Max Health	290
Armor	18
Speed	60
Critical Hit	60
Elemental Power	25

PERSONALITY FILE

A warrior at heart
Quick to learn
Nature-loving
Cheerful

Starting Powers

Attack 1

***TRAPTANIUM* AXE** Whacking evil left and right.

Attack 2

MYSTIC ACORN This nut will leave your enemies stunned.

Power Upgrades

500 Gold

HEADBASH Use your head to deliver broad damage.

900 Gold

IN A NUT SHELL Put on a new coat of nutshell armor to reduce damage.

700 Gold

NUT GRENADE Your Mystic Acorns now explode on impact!

1,200 Gold

THORN TRAIL Your *Traptanium* Axe leaves a trail of damaging thorns.

"Choose Your Path" Upgrades

Path 1: Axe Avenger Add some extra edge to your Axe attacks

1,700 Gold

AN AXE TO GRIND Your *Traptanium* Axe deals extra damage.

2,200 Gold

COMBO ATTACKS Combine attacks to spin and slash or slam enemies headfirst.

3,000 Gold

GO NUTS Shoot a barrage of acorns while you spin and slash.

Path 2: Armor Awesomeness Add extra layers of protective armor

1,700 Gold

BUSH'S SHACK Create a healing hut made of leaves.

2,200 Gold

PRIMAL WARRIOR More armor, extra damage.

3,000 Gold

SPRING FORWARD A quick dash and a Headbash.

AIR GUSTO

"GUSTS AND GLORY!"

Taught to control the wind by an ancient Cloud Dragon, Gusto stormed into action against a fleet of dragon hunters. They soon felt the back of his boomerang!

SOUL GEM
in Chompy Mountain

BOOMERANGS 4 BREAKFAST
Inhale and spit out your own boomerangs!

STARTING STATS	
Max Health	400
Armor	30
Speed	60
Critical Hit	50
Elemental Power	25

PERSONALITY FILE

- Jolly
- Loyal
- Full of surprises
- Has an appetite for fun

Starting Powers

Attack 1

***TRAPTANIUM* BOOMERANG** You'll never lose this weapon!

Attack 2

INHALER Suck 'em up and spit 'em out.

Power Upgrades

500 Gold

THE BREATH OF LIFE Inhaling enemies gives you a health boost.

900 Gold

ELECTRO-RANG Your boomerang attack gets an electrifying boost!

700 Gold

TWISTIN' IN THE WIND Spin that boomerang around and around.

1,200 Gold

LOTS OF LUNGPOWER Increase your appetite for enemies!

"Choose Your Path" Upgrades

Path 1: Air Ace Ramp up your 'rang skills

1,700 Gold

BOOM-ERANG Have a blast with your boomerang!

2,200 Gold

'RANG ME LIKE A HURRICANE Boomerang attacks bring mini-hurricanes.

3,000 Gold

BOOMERANG BUDDIES Surround yourself with spinning boomerangs.

Path 2: Dizzy Destroyer Putting the wind up your enemies!

1,700 Gold

SPIN LIKE THE WIND Twistin' in the Wind now comes with extra hurricanes.

2,200 Gold

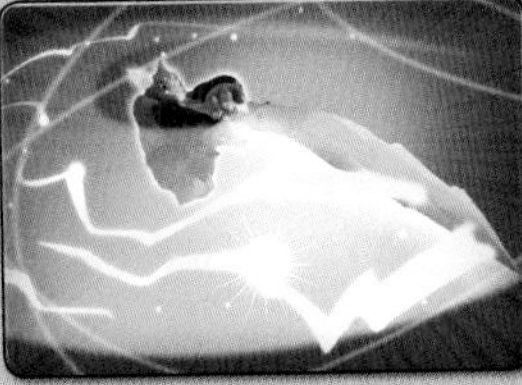

SHOCKING TWIST Add a little lightning to the mix.

3,000 Gold

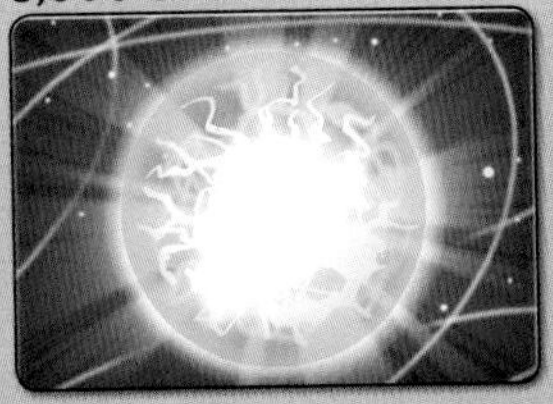

LIGHTNING BALL Transform into a ball of electrifying light.

AIR

THUNDERBOLT

"A STORM IS COMING!"

Wielding the magical Storm Sword, Thunderbolt saved Skylands from an eternal winter that put the Skylanders on ice. As a reward, he was made a member of the Trap Team.

SOUL GEM
in Time Town

LIGHTNING RAIN Rain never hurt anyone–until now!

STARTING STATS	
Max Health	410
Armor	48
Speed	60
Critical Hit	30
Elemental Power	25

PERSONALITY FILE

Stormy
Stoic
Competitive
Fearless

Starting Powers

Attack 1

***TRAPTANIUM* THUNDERSWORD** Storm into battle every time.

Attack 2

STORM CLOUDS Deluge foes with damage.

Power Upgrades

500 Gold

LIGHTNING CLOUDS Strike with electrified Storm Clouds.

900 Gold

MORE THUNDER The strength of your Storm Sword increases.

700 Gold

HURRICANE PAIN Let's twist again!

1,200 Gold

HURRICANE PAIN REMAINS Clouds are sucked into stronger hurricanes.

"Choose Your Path" Upgrades

Path 1: Power Conductor Amp up your Thundersword

1,700 Gold

DIRECT CURRENT Your sword delivers a lightning strike.

2,200 Gold

THUNDER THRUST A combo of calamitous proportions.

3,000 Gold

JUST ADD LIGHTNING There's nothing light about this lightning slam!

Path 2: I of the Storm An extreme weather warning!

1,700 Gold

STORMIER AND STORMIER Lightning strikes stretch farther.

2,200 Gold

CHARGE IT UP! Thundersword's attacks supercharge storm clouds.

3,000 Gold

EXPLODING CLOUDS Overload your storms for an explosive finish!

TECH

JAWBREAKER

"DOWN FOR THE COUNT!"

Jawbreaker was forced to fight Gear Trolls who wanted to turn his beloved Sky Train into an engine of evil. Putting his best fist forward, the righteous robot won the day.

SOUL GEM
in Soda Springs

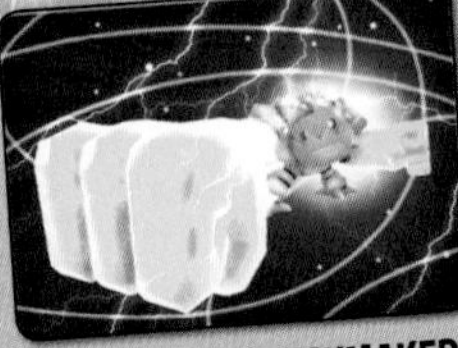

HYPERCHARGED HAYMAKER
Deliver a knockout blow!

STARTING STATS

Max Health	340
Armor	12
Speed	50
Critical Hit	70
Elemental Power	25

PERSONALITY FILE

Mechanical-minded
A unique thinker
Quick to act
Furious when provoked

Starting Powers

Attack 1

***TRAPTANIUM* PUNCH** The pick of the punch!

Attack 2

ROBO RAGE MODE Watch out! Jawbreaker's gone berserk!

Power Upgrades

500 Gold

RAGIN' ROBO RAGE Robo Rage rages on and on!

900 Gold

ALTERNATING CURRENT A Robo-rampage shocks enemies in more ways than one.

700 Gold

SPARK SHOCK Punch the ground to send sparks flying.

1,200 Gold

HEAVY HANDS Punches pack more, well, punch!

"Choose Your Path" Upgrades

Path 1: High Voltage Jab with extra jolts!

1,700 Gold

STATIC CLING Sparks stick to enemies. What a shock!

2,200 Gold

HANDS OFF! They hit you, they get hurt!

3,000 Gold

SPARKING INTEREST Robo Rage Mode makes continuous sparks.

Path 2: Out-RAGE-ous Become an even bigger hit!

1,700 Gold

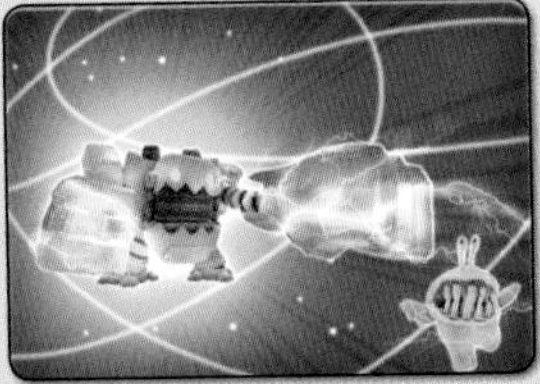

JOLTING JAB Static bursts blast more enemies.

2,200 Gold

DEFENSE FIRMWARE UPDATE Take less damage while raging!

3,000 Gold

PUNCH FOR POWER Punch longer and harder!

TECH

GEARSHIFT

"ALL GEARED UP!"

This mechanical princess preferred toiling in the mines to performing royal duties—but her father forgave her when she saved the Tech Kingdom of Metallana from Undead Stormriders.

SOUL GEM
in The Future of Skylands

SWING SHIFT Switch modes quicker with extra-strong gear!

STARTING STATS	
Max Health	300
Armor	24
Speed	70
Critical Hit	40
Elemental Power	25

PERSONALITY FILE
- Practical
- Humble
- Devoted
- Regal

Starting Powers

Attack 1

***TRAPTANIUM* GEAR** A technically brilliant attack.

Attack 2

MODE TOGGLE Switch between Hoop, Dual, or Fragment Mode.

Power Upgrades

500 Gold

GEAR GRIND Cartwheel forward, grinding anything in your path.

900 Gold

MANY MINI-GEARS Tiny Gears terrify enemy minions.

700 Gold

GEAR SAW Send a Gear Saw spinning.

1,200 Gold

MINI-GEAR DISTRIBUTION Hoop Mode blasts Mini-Gears into enemies.

"Choose Your Path" Upgrades

Path 1: Duel Mode Duelist Greater Gear Saws!

1,700 Gold

SPARE PARTS Duel Mode gets dangerous Gear Saws.

2,200 Gold

KEEP 'EM SPINNING Strike a Gear Saw and it'll spin longer.

3,000 Gold

GEARED UP Who ordered the king-size Gears?

Path 2: Fragment Mode Freak Your enemies will go to pieces!

1,700 Gold

ENHANCED FRAGMENTATION More fragments fling into the fray.

2,200 Gold

KICK IT INTO HIGH GEAR Mini-Gears from Fragment Mode? Yes, please!

3,000 Gold

HARDWARE OVERLOAD It's a Mini-Gear meltdown!

WALLOP

EARTH

"HAMMER IT HOME!"

Wallop spent centuries forging weapons on the anvils of Mount Scorch. However, his hammers were put to a different use the day he defended the volcano from a vicious Fire Viper.

SOUL GEM
in Chompy Mountain

NOW THAT'S A HAMMER!
Humongous hammers shall be yours!

STARTING STATS

Max Health	300
Armor	18
Speed	60
Critical Hit	50
Elemental Power	25

PERSONALITY FILE

- A good learner
- Tireless
- Skilled craftsman
- Prone to tantrums

Starting Powers

Attack 1

***TRAPTANIUM* HAMMER** Knock an enemy on the head.

Attack 2

HAMMER TOSS Throw a hammer, not a tantrum.

Power Upgrades

500 Gold

TANTRUM MODE Throw a tantrum, not a hammer!

900 Gold

WHEN HAMMERS COLLIDE Hammers spin and smash together!

700 Gold

HAMMER SLAMMER Each Hammer Toss brings more damage.

1,200 Gold

CUTTING EDGE Get super sledgehammers!

"Choose Your Path" Upgrades

Path 1: Tantrum Thrower Hammer your bad temper home!

1,700 Gold

INSTANT TANTRUM Fly into an instant rage.

2,200 Gold

TOTAL MELTDOWN A sure way for enemies to get totaled!

3,000 Gold

AFTERSHOCK WAVE Tantrums leave foes quaking!

Path 2: Hammer Handler Become a complete hammerhead!

1,700 Gold

BETTER WITH SHRAPNEL If I had a hammer, I'd blast you with shrapnel . . .

2,200 Gold

WHAT A COLLISION! Hammers collide with more force!

3,000 Gold

***TRAPTANIUM* SPLINTERS** Ouch! *Traptanium* shrapnel gets sticky!

EARTH

HEAD RUSH

"TAKING CHARGE!"

This brave warrior inspired her fellow villagers to rise up and overthrow the Harvest Sphinx who had them under her spell. She's always the first to rush forward!

SOUL GEM
in Wilikin Workshop

HORNS APLENTY Ultimate headgear unlocked!

STARTING STATS	
Max Health	340
Armor	48
Speed	60
Critical Hit	10
Elemental Power	25

PERSONALITY FILE
- Natural-born leader
- Inspirational
- Eager
- Optimistic

Starting Powers

Attack 1

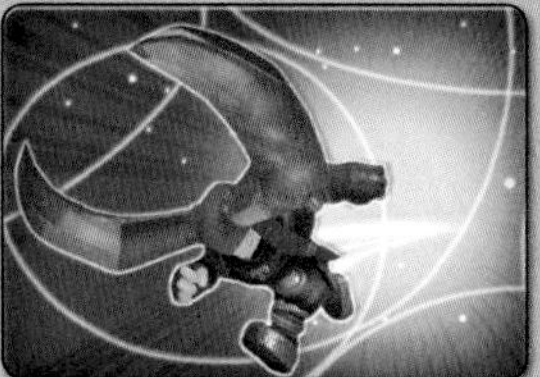

***TRAPTANIUM* HORNS** Leading the charge!

Attack 2

STOMP Stamp out enemies with every step.

Power Upgrades

500 Gold

MEGA STOMP Become even more heavy-footed.

900 Gold

STOMPING ON AIR Come crashing down with a super Stomp!

700 Gold

VODEL Yodel-ay-he-OW!

1,200 Gold

CHARGE CONTROL Twist and turn while charging!

"Choose Your Path" Upgrades

Path 1: Lungs of Steel Sing while you are winning!

1,700 Gold

HIGH NOTE Your souped-up solo brings more suffering!

2,200 Gold

MODULATE YODEL Pick the perfect pitch for destruction.

3,000 Gold

FORGET BREAKING GLASS Your chords churn the ground beneath your feet!

Path 2: Stomp Harder Stomp your way to success!

1,700 Gold

A STOMP TO REMEMBER They'll do more than hear you coming!

2,200 Gold

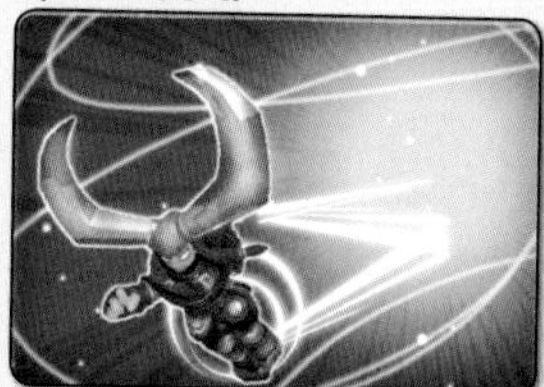

POWER STEERING Turning during a charge charges your turn.

3,000 Gold

OMEGA STOMP Crush evil underfoot once and for all!

KRYPT KING

"I'VE GOT THE EDGE!"

After wandering Skylands as a spirit, this ghostly knight took possession of a discarded Arkeyan suit of armor. He's been terrifying the forces of Darkness ever since!

STARTING STATS

Max Health	300
Armor	24
Speed	60
Critical Hit	40
Elemental Power	25

PERSONALITY FILE

Grave
Intimidating
Spirited
Valiant

SOUL GEM
in Monster Marsh

STORM SWORDS Super-sharp swords rain down on your enemies!

Starting Powers

Attack 1

***TRAPTANIUM* BROADSWORD** Your *Traptanium* sword is unsheathed.

Attack 2

THE SWARM Spray out undead insects that will bug enemies.

Power Upgrades

500 Gold

HAUNTED SWORD Your sword flies through the air. Literally!

900 Gold

THE BROADER THE BROADSWORD The sword is mightier than ever before.

700 Gold

SPECTRAL SLOWDOWN The Haunted Sword sends enemies into slow motion!

1,200 Gold

SUPER SWARM The bugs just got bigger!

"Choose Your Path" Upgrades

Path 1: Lord of the Sword Awesome attacks left, right, and center

1,700 Gold

ENCHANTED ARMOR Defeating foes increases your armor.

2,200 Gold

THE RICH GET RICHER Defeating foes increases your attacks, too!

3,000 Gold

COMBO ATTACKS Sabre Spin attack or Nether Blast? Your choice!

Path 2: Swarm Summoner This is a swarm warning!

1,700 Gold

STUNNING STING Your swarm gets a sting in the tail.

2,200 Gold

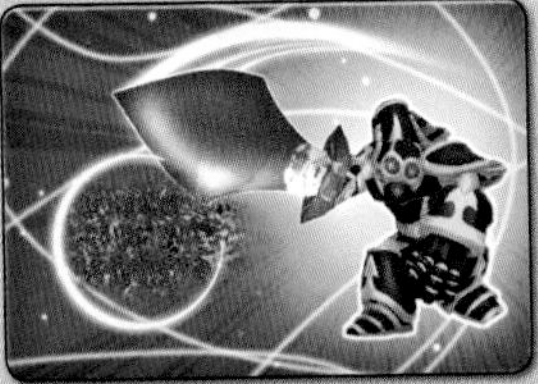

STIR UP THE SWARM A slice from your sword will power the swarm.

3,000 Gold

PARASITIC POWER Your swarm gains a healing touch!

UNDEAD

SHORT CUT

"CUT TO THE CHASE!"

When ordered to make magic clothes for pirates, this tricky tailor simply sewed the villains together. Now he cuts short the plans of evildoers everywhere.

SOUL GEM
in Lair of the Golden Queen

SCISSOR STILTS Cut a dash through enemy lines!

STARTING STATS

Max Health	280
Armor	18
Speed	70
Critical Hit	80
Elemental Power	25

PERSONALITY FILE

Creative
Crafty
Playful
Bit of a prankster

Starting Powers

Attack 1

***TRAPTANIUM* SCISSORS** Ready to cut evil down to size.

Attack 2

PHANTOM PUPPETS Mini marionettes menace minions.

Power Upgrades

500 Gold

CUTTING FRENZY Snip, snip, snippety-snip!

900 Gold

NO STRINGS ATTACHED Cut your puppets' strings to set them free.

700 Gold

NETHER NEEDLE Stich up enemies and draw them close.

1,200 Gold

CUT THROUGH WORLDS Snip open a rip in the fabric of time and space.

"Choose Your Path" Upgrades

Path 1: Scary Seamster You're sew dangerous!

1,700 Gold

TREACHEROUS TANGLE Tie enemies up in knots.

2,200 Gold

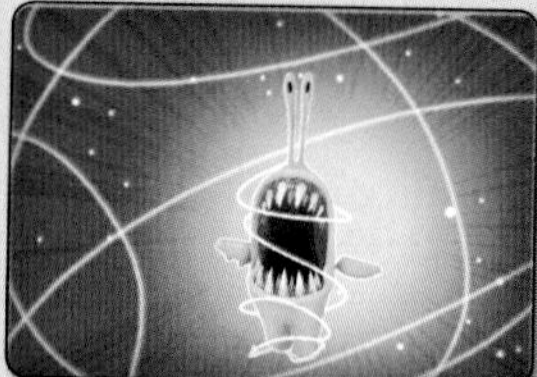

SUPER SNIPS Tangled enemies take more damage.

3,000 Gold

THREADSPLOSION Minions untangle only to explode!

Path 2: Puppet Master Become a Puppeteer of epic proportions

1,700 Gold

GO OUT WITH A BANG Phantom Puppets have a blast before vanishing.

2,200 Gold

PUPPET POPULATION Need more marionettes? Why knot!

3,000 Gold

PAGING DR. PUPPETS Your Puppets give you a health boost.

DARK

KNIGHT MARE

"NOWHERE TO HIDE!"

Ask the Oracle of Stones the wrong question and it will curse Skylands forever. Luckily, this Dark Centaur put her best hoof forward to stop a Bicyclops bunch from unleashing its terrible power.

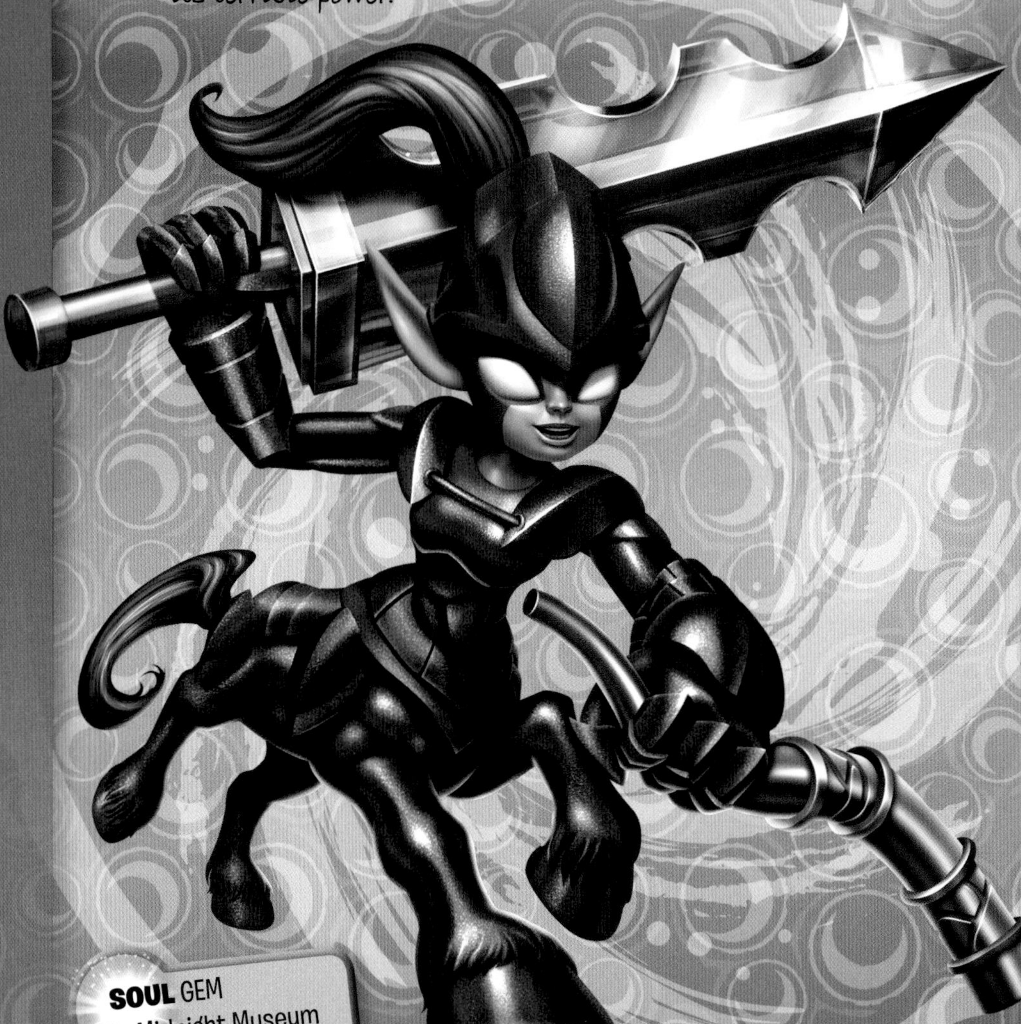

SOUL GEM
in Midnight Museum

THE SHADOW REALM Create a dark dimension where Shadowy Clones rule supreme!

STARTING STATS

Max Health	350
Armor	36
Speed	85
Critical Hit	40
Elemental Power	25

PERSONALITY FILE

Shadowy
Stubborn
Solitary
A skilled huntress

Starting Powers

Attack 1

***TRAPTANIUM* FLAMBERGE** A nightmare of a sword.

Attack 2

SHADOW JOUST Charge through enemies' defenses.

Power Upgrades

500 Gold

GIFT KEEPS ON GIVING Flamberge attacks bring long-lasting damage.

900 Gold

BATTLE HORN A blast on your horn leaves enemies stunned.

700 Gold

CHARGED-UP CHARGE Shadow Jousting gets more dangerous.

1,200 Gold

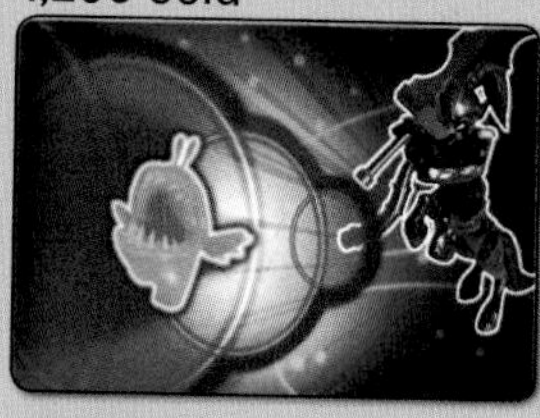

SHADOWY CLONES The Battle Horn summons a dark deadly double.

"Choose Your Path" Upgrades

Path 1: Shadow Summoner Have a blast with your Battle Horn

1,700 Gold

MORE CLONES Saddle up multiple Shadowy Clones.

2,200 Gold

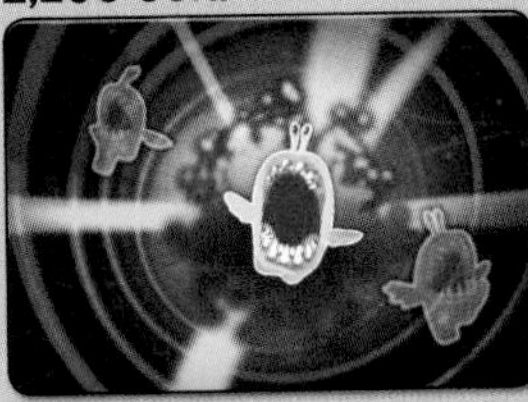

IT'S WIN-WIN! Clones explode, taking down enemies and healing you!

3,000 Gold

SHADOWY SACRIFICE Existing Shadowy Clones grant their power to new warriors!

Path 2: Flamberge Aficionado Fantastic Flamberge forever!

1,700 Gold

SHADOW STAB Have a stab at this crazy combo!

2,200 Gold

FLAMBERGE FRAGMENT Another combo, another night terror for your enemies.

3,000 Gold

SWORD OF DARKNESS The darkest of all Flamberge Swords is in your grasp!

LIGHT

KNIGHT LIGHT

"SEE THE LIGHT!"

When Luminous attacked Radiant City, Knight Light flew into action to protect the Starlight, a source of light, wisdom, and energy second only to the Core of Light itself.

SOUL GEM
in Sunscraper Spire

BRILLIANT BLADE Your *Traptanium* Scimitar blazes brighter than before!

STARTING STATS

Max Health	430
Armor	12
Speed	70
Critical Hit	70
Elemental Power	25

PERSONALITY FILE

Pure
Gallant
Illuminating
Righteous

Starting Powers

Attack 1

***TRAPTANIUM* SCIMITAR** There's nothing angelic about this sword.

Attack 2

PRISMATIC POUNCE A slash of the scimitar creates an aura of light.

Power Upgrades

500 Gold

HALLOWED GROUND Enemies bathed in light are slowed right down.

900 Gold

LASTING LIGHT Light auras are around longer.

700 Gold

LIGHT UP A circle of light levitates anything nearby.

1,200 Gold

SCHARPER SCIMITAR The *Traptanium* Scimitar reigns supreme.

"Choose Your Path" Upgrades

Path 1: Scimitar Slasher Master your shining sword

1,700 Gold

ASCENDING STRIKE Send your enemies flying with a single strike.

2,200 Gold

SPEED OF LIGHT Teleport up high to come down hard.

3,000 Gold

SPINNING SLASH An all-around attack.

Path 2: Luminary of Light Walk the path of light

1,700 Gold

RADIANT RADIUS Auras shed more light.

2,200 Gold

ILLUMINATION DETONATION Auras bring light explosions.

3,000 Gold

FLASH DASH Become a vision of invulnerability.

MEET THE SKYLANDERS

MAGIC

DÉJÀ VU

"DID THAT JUST HAPPEN?"

Caught in a timestorm while protecting her island from Giant Sea Slugs, Déjà Vu is always on the clock when it comes to fighting evil.

SOUL GEM
in Rainfish Riviera

BLACK HOLE BEDLAM Time Rifts transform into unstable black holes.

STARTING STATS

Max Health	210
Armor	18
Speed	60
Critical Hit	60
Elemental Power	25

PERSONALITY FILE

Intelligent
Hardworking
Quick thinker
Always on time

Starting Powers

Attack 1

SPACE-TIME SHOTS Fire a homing ball of pure time energy.

Attack 2

PAST SELVES Bring back your past self–and then blow it up!

Power Upgrades

500 Gold

TIME RIFT Create a rift in time that's one step away from a black hole.

900 Gold

TIME RIFTS APLENTY Multiple Time Rifts attract Space-Time Shots.

700 Gold

LONG-TERM MEMORY Past Selves repeat history for longer.

1,200 Gold

CIRCULAR LOGIC Past Selves can now fire upon enemies.

"Choose Your Path" Upgrades

Path 1: Remember to Live Take control of time!

1,700 Gold

EXPLOSION DÉJÀ VU Past Self detonations are repeated time and time again.

2,200 Gold

TIME HEALS ALL WOUNDS When Past Selves are damaged, you are healed!

3,000 Gold

SPACE-TIME DUALITY Two Space-Time Shots at the same time.

Path 2: Live to Remember Your past catches up with your enemies!

1,700 Gold

WARP FIELD Shooting a Past Self drags enemies toward it!

2,200 Gold

PAST SELF PARALYSIS Your Past Selves freeze time for your foes.

3,000 Gold

GO OUT WITH A BANG Past Selves shoot Space-Time Shots when they explode.

MAGIC

COBRA CADABRA

"CHARMED AND READY!"

You'll be charmed, I'm sure, by this master magician, a member of the Mysteriously Mad Magic Masters of Mystery, no less!

SOUL GEM
in Operation: Troll Rocket Steal

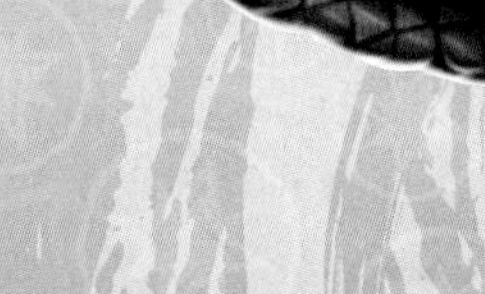

BIG BASKET BOMB The biggest basket blast of all.

STARTING STATS

Max Health	290
Armor	36
Speed	70
Critical Hit	40
Elemental Power	25

PERSONALITY FILE

Master illusionist
Never what he seems
Musical
Tricky

Starting Powers

Attack 1

MAGIC FLUTE Your Magic Pungi Flute delivers more than just tunes.

Attack 2

COBRA BASKET Throw snake baskets at slippery customers.

Power Upgrades

500 Gold

KEEP THE BEAT! Fire your flute to the beat of the music.

900 Gold

BASKET PARTY Control up to five serpents at once.

700 Gold

LAUNCH COBRA Blast yourself from your own Cobra Basket.

1,200 Gold

PUNGI POWER Your flute jumps up a scale.

"Choose Your Path" Upgrades

Path 1: Concerto Cobra Make magical music

1,700 Gold

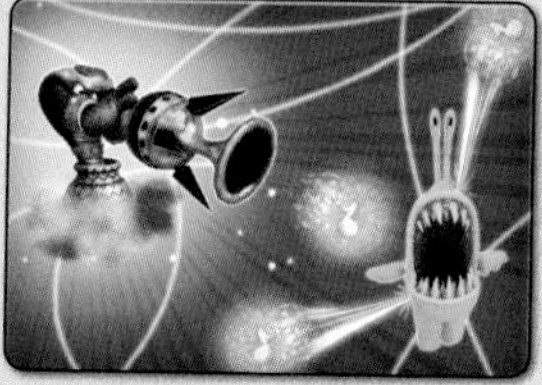

REVERB RIFF Musical notes ricochet off walls.

2,200 Gold

ULTIMATE FLUTE ROCK Rock your enemies to their knees.

3,000 Gold

SNAKE CHARMER'S SOLO Charm your foe to fight on the side of right.

Path 2: Master of Baskets Become a basket case!

1,700 Gold

BASKET QUINTET Throw a trio of baskets. Not enough? Then take five!

2,200 Gold

CALL AND RESPONSE Baskets get bonus powers when shot by your song.

3,000 Gold

A-TISKET, A-TASKET Blow up every active basket.

WATER ECHO

"LET'S MAKE SOME NOISE!"

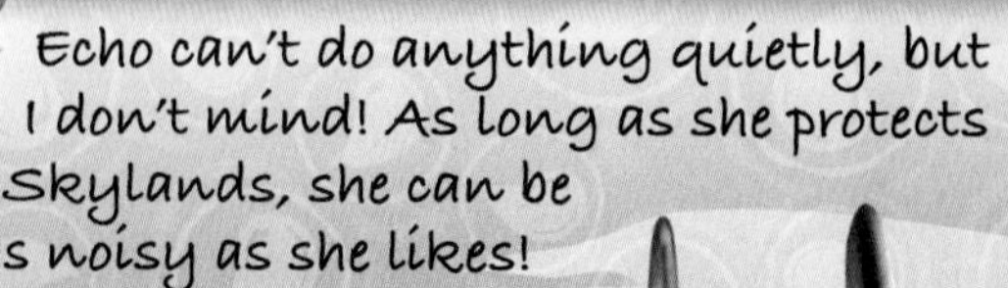

Echo can't do anything quietly, but I don't mind! As long as she protects Skylands, she can be as noisy as she likes!

SOUL GEM
in Secret Sewers of Supreme Stink

CALL OF THE SIREN Using a Siren Song in a bubble puts attacker in a trance!

STARTING STATS	
Max Health	270
Armor	42
Speed	50
Critical Hit	20
Elemental Power	25

PERSONALITY FILE
- Music lover
- Lively
- Enthusiastic
- Loud and proud

Starting Powers

Attack 1

SIREN SCREAM Your enemies will feel the noise!

Attack 2

BUBBLE BOMBS Make explosive bubbles that bounce to the beat.

Power Upgrades

500 Gold

SONIC SLAM Beat the eardrums–it's body-slam time!

900 Gold

4-BEAT Four times the Bubble Bombs!

700 Gold

PITCH CONTROL Hold your notes longer, causing more damage.

1,200 Gold

SUBSONIC Sonic Slam aftershocks all the way!

"Choose Your Path" Upgrades

Path 1: Bubble Up! I'm forever blowing up bubbles . . .

1,700 Gold

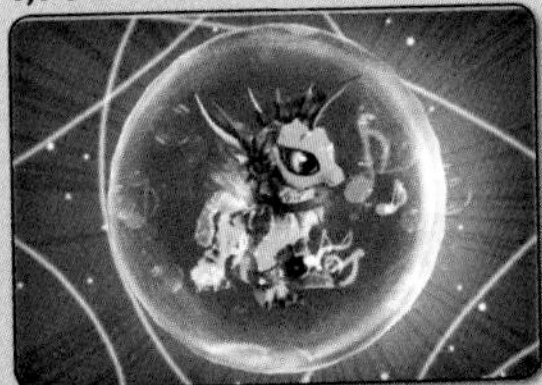

BUBBLE SHIELD Blow a protective bubble around yourself.

2,200 Gold

POWER POP Bubble Bombs hit the top of the charts.

3,000 Gold

BURST MY BUBBLE Explode your Bubble Shield near enemies.

Path 2: Singalong Sing with power!

1,700 Gold

ULTIMATE PITCH CONTROL It's the song that goes on and on!

2,200 Gold

SCREAM OUT Time for the last shout!

3,000 Gold

ULTRASOUND Charge up the Sonic Slam for an ear-popping echo!

WATER

FLIP WRECK

"MAKING WAVES!"

Flip Wreck became a Skylander after saving the playful dolphins of Bottlenose Bay from an Ice Viking attack.

SOUL GEM
in Mystic Mill

SEA SLAMMERIN Ride in on a Wheel Shield and land a super slam!

STARTING STATS

Max Health	300
Armor	30
Speed	60
Critical Hit	30
Elemental Power	25

PERSONALITY FILE

- Adventurous
- Single-minded
- Curious
- Adaptable

Starting Powers

Attack 1

SEA SAW Swing your saw sword at enemies.

Attack 2

WHEELING AND DEALING Ride a ship steering wheel shield to cause damage.

Power Upgrades

500 Gold

WHEEL SHIELD BASH Bash your enemies with the Wheel Shield.

900 Gold

SUPER SEA SAW Increase the damage of your saw sword.

700 Gold

SPLASH DAMAGE Use your blowhole to deliver a big blast.

1,200 Gold

SHIELD MODE Become temporarily invincible.

"Choose Your Path" Upgrades

Path 1: Fish Commander Wheel and Deal like never before

1,700 Gold

FISH?! Release an army of fish from your Wheel Shield.

2,200 Gold

HOMING FISH Your fish will auto-zoom directly to your enemies.

3,000 Gold

ENDLESS FISH Release an endless stream of fighting fish.

Path 2: Sword Specialist Learn some new Sea Saw tricks

1,700 Gold

SWORD SWELLS Send a torrent of water from your Saw.

2,200 Gold

SEA SAW COMBOS Learn to make a Whirlpool or cause an Undersea Ambush.

3,000 Gold

BLOWHOLE BLASTER Increase the damage and range of your blowhole attack.

FIRE

TORCH

"FIRE IT UP!"

When her village was trapped in a giant glacier, Torch built a Firespout Flamethrower to defeat the Snow Dragon behind the enchanted frost. Now she searches for the grandfather she lost on that fateful day . . .

SOUL GEM
in Mystic Mill

THE INCINERATOR The ultimate flamethrower in your hands!

STARTING STATS

Max Health	230
Armor	12
Speed	60
Critical Hit	40
Elemental Power	25

PERSONALITY FILE

- Fears nothing
- Fiery
- Alert
- Swift

Starting Powers

Attack 1

BLAZING BELLOW Throw flames at any enemy.

Attack 2

FLAMING HORSESHOES Anything but lucky for enemies they strike.

Power Upgrades

500 Gold

HEATING UP Flamethrowers shoot farther and cause more fire damage.

900 Gold

PYRO PENDANT Flaming Horseshoes turn up the heat.

700 Gold

FLAMING HAIR WHIP The hottest hairstyle in Skylands.

1,200 Gold

BLUE FLAME Singed enemies will be left feeling blue.

"Choose Your Path" Upgrades

Path 1: Forged in Flames Fan those flames!

1,700 Gold

SCORCHED EARTH POLICY Flamethrowers set the ground alight.

2,200 Gold

HAIR'S GETTING LONG Your flaming hairdo does more damage.

3,000 Gold

DOUBLE BARREL BELLOWS Twice the burn!

Path 2: Maid of Metal Do the hot shoe shuffle!

1,700 Gold

EXTRA HOT SHOES There's no horsing around with these shoes!

2,200 Gold

FIREWORKS DISPLAY Horseshoes go bang when they go out.

3,000 Gold

HOPPING MAD HORSESHOES Flaming Horseshoes burst into life!

FIRE

TRAIL BLAZER

"THE MANE EVENT!"

The hottest-tempered unicorn in Skylands, Trail Blazer's fury burns deep whenever he sees injustice at work.

SOUL GEM
in The Future of Skylands

HEAT WAVE Release a scorching wave of fire.

STARTING STATS	
Max Health	270
Armor	18
Speed	85
Critical Hit	30
Elemental Power	25

PERSONALITY FILE
- Just
- Volatile
- Hot-footed
- Filled with fury

Starting Powers

Attack 1

FIREBALL Fling flame from your horn!

Attack 2

ROUNDHOUSE KICK Kick out at your enemies!

Power Upgrades

500 Gold

BRING THE HEAT Fireballs get a boost.

900 Gold

BUCKING BRONCO Kick everyone at once!

700 Gold

STAMPEDE! Lead a furious charge.

1,200 Gold

FUEL THE FIRE Every attack carries extra damage.

"Choose Your Path" Upgrades

Path 1: Equine Excellence The stampede supreme!

1,700 Gold

FLAMING FORMS Get two burning buddies as you stampede.

2,200 Gold

FIREWALKER Leave a trail of red-hot hoofprints.

3,000 Gold

TRIPLE FIREBALLS The clue is in the name!

Path 2: Fireballer Flame on!

1,700 Gold

KICK IT UP A NOTCH Kick with even more passion.

2,200 Gold

BOUNCING FIREBALLS Flame flies farther than before.

3,000 Gold

NOT HIS FIRST RODEO Be a Bucking Bronco longer!

LIFE

FOOD FIGHT

"EAT THIS!"

Here's a Skylander who was never told not to play with his food. And you thought fruit and veggies were good for you!

SOUL GEM
in Know-It-All Island

THAT'S HOW I ROLL Squash your enemies beneath a giant tomato!

STARTING STATS

Max Health	260
Armor	18
Speed	60
Critical Hit	30
Elemental Power	25

PERSONALITY FILE

Veggie lover
Always fresh-faced
Ready for action
A heart of gold

Starting Powers

Attack 1

TOMATO LAUNCHER Pulp your foes with fresh tomatoes.

Attack 2

BLOOMS OF DOOM Trap enemies in an artichoke trap–and then blow them up!

Power Upgrades

500 Gold

EXTRA-RIPE TOMATOES You say tomato, I say AAAAAAARGH!

900 Gold

ZUCCHINI BLAST What's more dangerous than a tomato? A Zucchini, obviously.

700 Gold

GREEN THUMB Tomatoes turn into power-boosting plants.

1,200 Gold

BLOOMS OF BIGGER DOOM Your Doom Blooms bloom into bigger booms.

"Choose Your Path" Upgrades

Path 1: Tomatologist Add a little sauce to your tomato plants.

1,700 Gold

HEAVY HARVEST Tomato plants give a bumper crop.

2,200 Gold

HEIRBOOM TOMATOES Zucchini Blasts cause tomato plants to explode.

3,000 Gold

BAD AFTERTASTE Minions mashed by Tomato plants continue taking damage.

Path 2: Bloomer and Boomer Championship Zucchinis will be yours!

1,700 Gold

SPECIAL SQUASH Zucchini Blasts get more zip.

2,200 Gold

ZUCCHINI GOO Enemies forced to snack on Zucchini slow right down.

3,000 Gold

'CHOKE CHAIN Blooms of Doom set each other off!

LIFE

HIGH FIVE

"BUZZ OFF!"

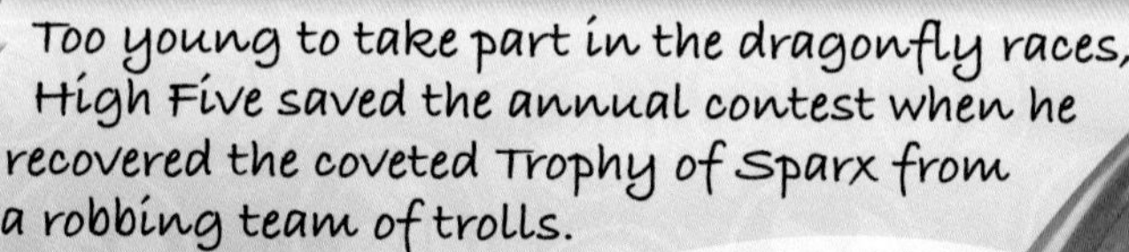

Too young to take part in the dragonfly races, High Five saved the annual contest when he recovered the coveted Trophy of Sparx from a robbing team of trolls.

STARTING STATS

Max Health	270
Armor	6
Speed	60
Critical Hit	70
Elemental Power	25

PERSONALITY FILE

Always dashing around

Short attention span

Wants to be involved

Impulsive

SOUL GEM

in Secret Sewers of Supreme Stink

ORGANIC SLAM APPLES Fly Slam fruit is even better for you.

Starting Powers

Attack 1

POISON PELLETS There are no flies on this fast-acting attack.

Attack 2

BUZZ DASH Sorry, must dash!

Power Upgrades

500 Gold

POISON CLOUD Enemies will want to miss this purple poisonous mist.

900 Gold

BUZZ CHARGE Speed even faster into action!

700 Gold

FLY SLAM Incoming insect! Perfect the perfect body slam.

1,200 Gold

BUZZERKER OVERDRIVE Standing beneath a Fly Slamming Dragonfly? Are you crazy?

"Choose Your Path" Upgrades

Path 1: Pollen Prince Every cloud has a poisonous lining

1,700 Gold

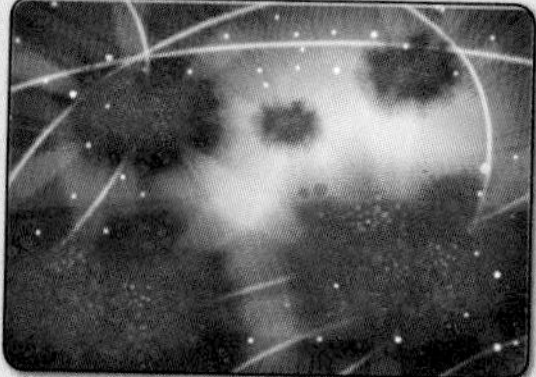

CLOUD CONTROL Have up to five Poison Clouds floating around at once.

2,200 Gold

BUZZ 'EM UP Dash through your Clouds to make them hang around longer.

3,000 Gold

POWER CLOUDS Colossal Clouds crammed with poison.

Path 2: Speedy Slammer Dash to it!

1,700 Gold

SPIN CYCLE Pull enemies into your Fly Slam.

2,200 Gold

BUZZ BUZZ BUZZ Make one Buzz Dash after another.

3,000 Gold

SLAM APPLES Fly Slams produce healing apples. Handy!

AIR

FLING KONG

"MONKEY SEE, MONKEY DOOM!"

This master of Monk-Ru defeated the foul-smelling Gorilla-Goos when they tried to steal a mystical monkey idol. Now he puts his air-powered martial arts to good use, knocking the wind out of minions.

SOUL GEM
in Wilikin Workshop

MAKE IT RAIN Power Discs fly down from above.

STARTING STATS

Max Health	240
Armor	12
Speed	70
Critical Hit	70
Elemental Power	25

PERSONALITY FILE

Cheeky
Precise
Swift
Always in a rush

Starting Powers

Attack 1

POWER DISCS Send your Vortex Discs spinning

Attack 2

MAGIC CARPET DASH Take a Magic Carpet ride.

Power Upgrades

500 Gold

SPIKED Make a point with these spiked discs.

900 Gold

MAD DASH Fly faster and longer. No monkeying around!

700 Gold

CYMBAL CRASH Smashing Power Discs together sends out shockwaves.

1,200 Gold

THE KONG KLANG Enemies are stunned by your calamitous cymbals.

"Choose Your Path" Upgrades

Path 1: Disc Jockey It's total disc destruction!

1,700 Gold

TRICK SHOT Vortex Discs fly straight through Villains and bounce off walls.

2,200 Gold

SMASH HITS Make some noise with this carpet-cymbal combo!

3,000 Gold

A TOSS-UP Go over the top with an overarm fling.

Path 2: Carpet Captain Ramp up your magic rug!

1,700 Gold

SMASH 'N' DASH Hitting enemies gives you a flying boost.

2,200 Gold

DOUBLE WHAMMY The combo of choice if you want two flying discs.

3,000 Gold

SHOCK TREATMENT Your Magic Carpet Dash leaves a trail of shocking electricity.

AIR BLADES

"LOOKING SHARP!"

Originally terrified of the Golden Fear Serpent, Blades conquered his fears to banish the monster forever. I rewarded such bravery by making Blades a Skylander!

SOUL GEM
in Soda Springs

INSTANT SWIRL SHARDS
Cyclone Swirls contain Blade Shards galore.

STARTING STATS

Max Health	280
Armor	30
Speed	60
Critical Hit	10
Elemental Power	25

PERSONALITY FILE

- Courageous
- Gutsy
- Single-minded
- Steadfast

Starting Powers

Attack 1

WING SLICE Beat your enemies with your steel-like wings.

Attack 2

BLADE SHARDS Shoot steel shards from your wings.

Power Upgrades

500 Gold

CYCLONE SWIRL Twist your enemies around your little finger–or at least your wings.

900 Gold

SHARD HARDER More shards than ever before.

700 Gold

SHARPENED WINGS Slice through the air with new sharpened wings.

1,200 Gold

WIND AT YOUR BACK Your Cyclone Swirl now follows you into battle.

"Choose Your Path" Upgrades

Path 1: Wind Wielder The wind is changing

1,700 Gold

FOLLOW LIKE THE WIND Cyclone Swirls stay close while Blade Shards get faster.

2,200 Gold

CRUSHING CYCLONES Foes trapped in your twisters take on extra damage.

3,000 Gold

SHIELDING SWIRL Cyclones swell in size to see off enemy firepower.

Path 2: Shard Shooter Boost your Blade Shards

1,700 Gold

SLICE SHARDS Wing Slices shoot out Blade Shards from time to time.

2,200 Gold

CUTTING EDGE Blade Shards get sharper still.

3,000 Gold

SHARD SHRAPNEL Blade Shards stick to enemies like glue. Sharp, pointy glue, at that!

TECH 

TREAD HEAD

"TREAD AND SHRED!"

Competing in the race of his life, Tread Head threw away the lead to save his fellow racers from a Goblin roadblock. Such self-sacrifice made this speed freak perfect Skylander material.

SOUL GEM
in Mystic Mill

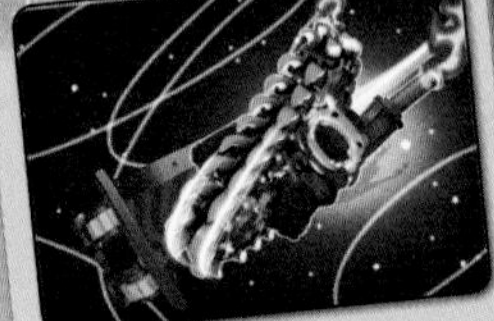

ROCKET BOOST Perform a daredevil jump off a rocketing ramp.

STARTING STATS

Max Health	270
Armor	18
Speed	85
Critical Hit	20
Elemental Power	25

PERSONALITY FILE

- Has a need for speed
- Inventive
- Unselfish
- Plucky

Starting Powers

Attack 1

WHEELIE Pop a Wheelie to push enemies aside.

Attack 2

BACKFIRE BLAST Look out behind you!

Power Upgrades

500 Gold

PEDAL TO THE METAL Wheelies last a *wheelie* long time.

900 Gold

TREAD HEAVILY Bigger treads mean bigger dread from foes.

700 Gold

SPIN OUT Go into a skid to take less damage.

1,200 Gold

KICK UP SOME DUST Spin Outs leave your enemies spinning, too!

"Choose Your Path" Upgrades

Path 1: Drag Racer Give your treads a tune-up!

1,700 Gold

SPIKE A WHEELIE Get a grip of the road with super-sharp spikes.

2,200 Gold

GO OUT WITH A BANG The biggest backfire of them all.

3,000 Gold

BURNING RUBBER Leave a burning trail that will trip up your foes.

Path 2: Pavement Peeler Spin to win!

1,700 Gold

EAT MY DUST Spin Outs slow enemies to a crawl.

2,200 Gold

SPRAY IT, DON'T SAY IT Pull a tight Wheelie Turn to kick up the dirt.

3,000 Gold

FIRE SPIN Spin Outs burn up the ground.

TECH

CHOPPER

"DINO MIGHT!"

Smaller than the rest of his dinosaur tribe, Chopper built himself a Gyro-Dino-Exo-Suit. A volcano erupted during its test flight, but Chopper flew into the inferno to rescue his bigger brothers and sisters.

SOUL GEM
in Chef Zeppelin

ULTIMATE DINO DESTRUCTION Fire rockets from the air.

STARTING STATS

Max Health	250
Armor	6
Speed	60
Critical Hit	50
Elemental Power	25

PERSONALITY FILE

Never says never
Aims sky-high
Genius inventor
Trustworthy

Starting Powers

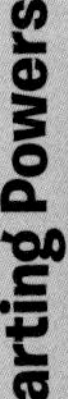

Attack 1

RAPTOR ROCKETS Missiles with real bite!

Attack 2

CHOPPER BLADES Charge with blades down to cut through enemies.

Power Upgrades

500 Gold

ROAR You may be small, but you've got a big voice.

900 Gold

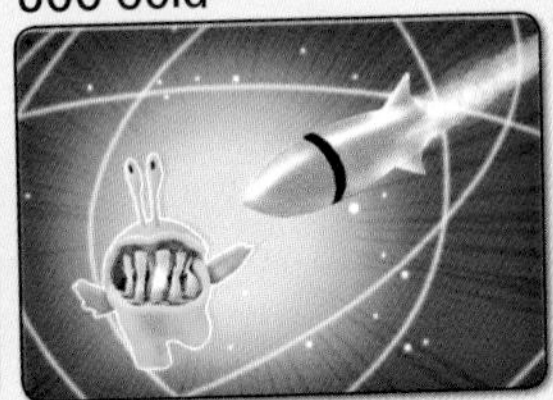

HOMING MISSILES Seek and destroy enemies wherever they are.

700 Gold

REV'D UP ROCKETS Rockets give more bang for your buck.

1,200 Gold

BETTER BLADES These righteous rotors will take you for a spin.

"Choose Your Path" Upgrades

Path 1: Roar Like Never Before Get more roar!

1,700 Gold

CALL OF THE WILD Just when you thought your roar couldn't get louder.

2,200 Gold

R.O.A.R MISSILES The ultimate in Dino-Might-Rage of All Raptor missiles.

3,000 Gold

KING OF THE JURASSIC JUNGLE A screaming roar that is off the scale.

Path 2: Blast from the Past Boom, boom, shake the room!

1,700 Gold

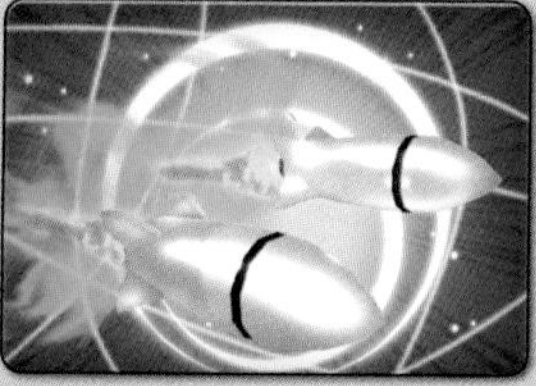

THE BIGGER THE BOOM Your explosions not big enough? Here's the solution.

2,200 Gold

PROPS TO YOU The ultimate Chopper Blade attack.

3,000 Gold

MORE MISSILES Still not happy with your rockets? Then try these on for size.

EARTH

ROCKY ROLL

"ROLL WITH IT!"

Rocky the rock digger and Roll the boulder have known each other since mining school. Friends to the core, the stony-faced duo now brings evildoers down to Earth all over Skylands.

SOUL GEM
in Time Town

BOULDER POSSE The bigger Boulder Barrier imaginable.

STARTING STATS

Max Health	270
Armor	30
Speed	60
Critical Hit	40
Elemental Power	25

PERSONALITY FILE

- Like-minded
- Team players
- Dreamers
- Adventurous

Starting Powers

Attack 1

SPIT BALL *Ptooey!* Roll rolls out a bouncing boulder.

Attack 2

BOULDER DASH Rocky runs forward on Roll's back.

Power Upgrades

500 Gold

BOULDER BARRIER A protective ring of boulders rolls into place.

900 Gold

BOUNCY ATTACK MODE Give your Boulder Barriers a little bounce.

700 Gold

ROCK ON Ball and Dash attacks bring more damage.

1,200 Gold

MOH BOULDERS Boulder Barriers get more crowded.

"Choose Your Path" Upgrades

Path 1: Geological Grandmaster Roll up, roll up for better boulders!

1,700 Gold

SUPER SPIT BALL Roll spits out monster boulders.

2,200 Gold

ROCK HARDEST Rocky Roll attacks to the max!

3,000 Gold

TRIPLE SPIT BALLS Spit out three boulders that break into smaller stones.

Path 2: Rolling Rumbler Dash dukes it out!

1,700 Gold

LET'S ROLL A rolling stone gathers more speed!

2,200 Gold

ROLL WITH THE PUNCHES Roll delivers an earth-shattering punch!

3,000 Gold

ROCKY BOXING This upgrade's a real knockout.

EARTH

FIST BUMP

"KNOCK, KNOCK . . . TOO LATE!"

When Greebles built a new base in the Bubbling Bamboo Forest, Fist Bump shook the building site to its foundations with a single punch! No wonder Terrafin advised me to make him a Skylander!

SOUL GEM
in Monster Marsh

RIDING THE RAILS Create mini Fault Lines just by walking!

STARTING STATS	
Max Health	280
Armor	30
Speed	60
Critical Hit	20
Elemental Power	25

PERSONALITY FILE
Bold
Confident
Thick-skinned
One of a kind

Starting Powers

Attack 1

PANDA POUND Smashing the ground activates Fault Lines.

Attack 2

FAULT LINE SLAM This time the bash creates Fault Lines. Don't blame us!

Power Upgrades

500 Gold

SEISMIC SLIDE Slip-slide into your enemies. It's ramming time!

900 Gold

HOLD THE LINE Fault Lines spread out farther.

700 Gold

PANQUAKE Pound the ground to create even more fearsome Fault Lines.

1,200 Gold

DON'T BUMP FIST BUMP Fault Lines erupt when you get hit. It's your foes' fault, really!

"Choose Your Path" Upgrades

Path 1: Rowdy Richer Make better quakes!

1,700 Gold

FAULT LINES IN GLASS HOUSES Some Fault Lines shoot stones at minions!

2,200 Gold

QUAKE 'N' BAKE Activated Fault Lines get more awesome.

3,000 Gold

A BOLDER BOULDER Spiky stones shoot out of Fault Lines.

Path 2: Bamboo Bonanza Perfect Panda Pounds every time!

1,700 Gold

HEALING BAMBOO Some Fault Lines produce health-giving bamboo shoots.

2,200 Gold

BAMBOO HARVEST Panda Pound in midair to make Bamboo Plants Bam-BOOM!

3,000 Gold

JUMP FOR IT Create extra Fault Lines when you Panda Pound in the air.

FUNNY BONE

"I HAVE A BONE TO PICK!"

Funny Bone came from Punch Line Island, but soon discovered that protecting the Chuckling Trees was no laughing matter. Now he makes evil laugh on the other side of its face.

SOUL GEM
in The Phoenix Psanctuary

HEALING PAWS Bone Paws give a healing pat to perk you up.

STARTING STATS

Max Health	270
Armor	24
Speed	70
Critical Hit	20
Elemental Power	25

PERSONALITY FILE

Bit of a prankster
Laughs a lot
Always burying things
Never bone-idle

Starting Powers

Attack 1

FLYING BONE DISC Fling a flying Disc of bony doom.

Attack 2

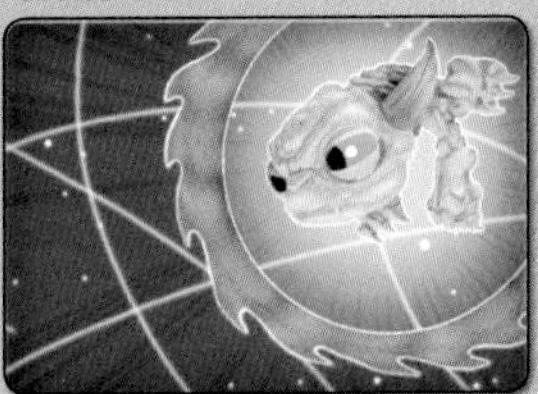

BONE SAW Enemies cut down by this attack are just *saw* losers!

Power Upgrades

500 Gold

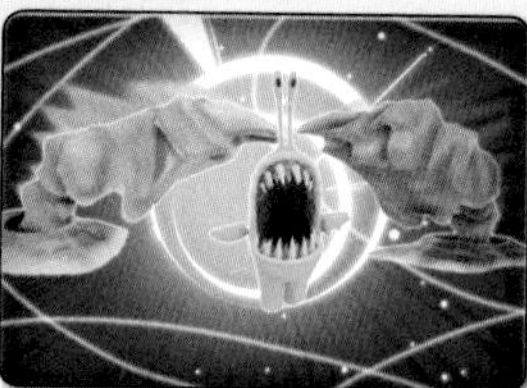

BONE PAWS Giant Bone Paws from the grave grab enemies.

900 Gold

FEROCIOUS FETCH Grab your Discs in your gnashers.

700 Gold

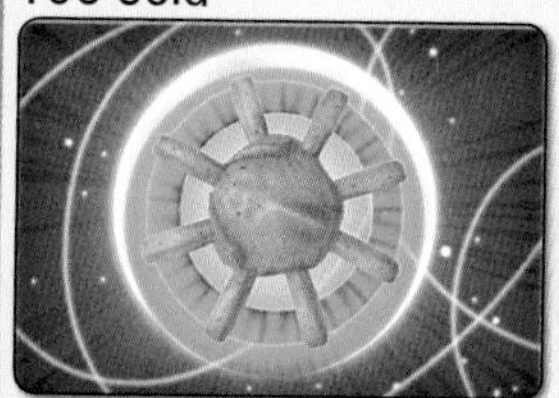

DISC DEMON Own better Bone Discs!

1,200 Gold

BUMP UP THE BLADES Charge the Bone Saw for an extra dangerous dash!

"Choose Your Path" Upgrades

Path 1: Tail Wagger You are the bone and only!

1,700 Gold

SUPERCHARGED SAW The Bone Saw just keeps getting better and better.

2,200 Gold

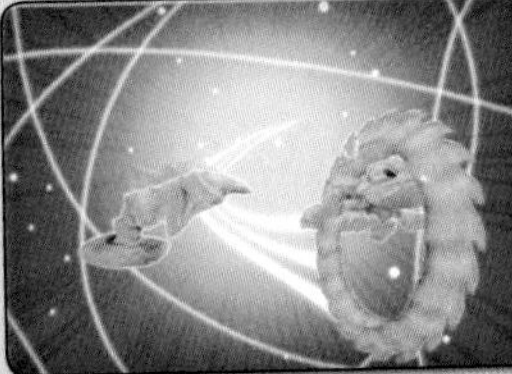

BONE PAW POWER Your ground defenses give the Bone Saw a helping paw.

3,000 Gold

HEAD CASE A spectral skull snacks on enemies during Saw attacks.

Path 2: Bone Zoner The finest Flying Bone Discs in all of Skylands

1,700 Gold

FLYING BONE BOOM Bone Discs now go boom, boom, boom!

2,200 Gold

ULTIMATE FBD Slamming a Bone Disc causes absolute chaos.

3,000 Gold

PLAY CATCH Bone Paws chuck Flying Bone Discs around!

BAT SPIN

"NO REST FOR THE WICKED!"

After losing her undead relatives, Bat Spin was raised by a family of magical bats. She first entered my radar when she saved her batty brothers and sisters from invading Undead trolls.

SOUL GEM
in Telescope Towers

GREAT BALL OF BATS
Summon a swirling ball of biting bats.

STARTING STATS

Max Health	240
Armor	12
Speed	85
Critical Hit	50
Elemental Power	25

PERSONALITY FILE

Scary
Good listener
Loves her pets
Never gets in a flap

Starting Powers

Attack 1

BAT ATTACK Your pets will drive enemies batty!

Attack 2

BAT SWARM Whip up a storm of spectral bats.

Power Upgrades

500 Gold

HEALING BITE Bats that munch on minions give you a health boost.

900 Gold

GO BATTY! Transform into a terrifying giant bat!

700 Gold

BRAWNY BATS Your bats fly longer and attack more!

1,200 Gold

A COLONY OF BATS Get an entire army of flying bats.

"Choose Your Path" Upgrades

Path 1: Pet Purveyor Get a new bunch of bats!

1,700 Gold

MR. DIZZY Foes will find your crazy new bat confusing!

2,200 Gold

MR. BLOCKY This brave bat blocks you from enemy fire.

3,000 Gold

MR. BITEY No one bites, nibbles, and chews like Mr. Bitey!

Path 2: Bat Betterment Be the best bat you can be!

1,700 Gold

BAT-TLE CRY Get a new sonic screech in Bat Form!

2,200 Gold

ULTIMATE BAT SQUAD Bat buddies fly on your wing.

3,000 Gold

CHIROPTERAN CALL Shoot out three bats with every bite!

DARK

BLACKOUT

"DARKNESS FALLS!"

The Dark Stygian Dragon Clan spread nightmares across Skylands. Even I couldn't sleep until Blackout banished my bad dreams—and his former Clan brothers—forever.

SOUL GEM
in Know-It-All Island

SUPERNOVA BLACK HOLE
Combine two Black Holes to create a dark Supernova!

STARTING STATS

Max Health	260
Armor	24
Speed	60
Critical Hit	40
Elemental Power	25

PERSONALITY FILE

Mysterious
Shadowy
Intimidating
Unfathomable

Starting Powers

Attack 1

WING WHIP Whip enemies into a frenzy with your wicked wings.

Attack 2

SHADOW ORBS Your sinister spheres leave foes in the dark.

Power Upgrades

500 Gold

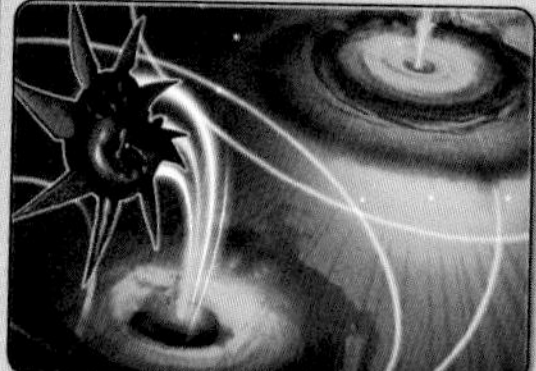

BLACK HOLE Teleport yourself–or your enemies–through Black Holes.

900 Gold

SHADOW BLADE Become a spinning black blade.

700 Gold

DARKNESS OVERLOAD Black Holes explode if shot by a Shadow Orb.

1,200 Gold

TAKE IT BLACK Black Holes keep hold of foes longer.

"Choose Your Path" Upgrades

Path 1: Wing Warrior The darkest of shadows will be yours

1,700 Gold

A SPINNING FINISH Spin into these Shadow Blade combos.

2,200 Gold

WHIP IT UP All your attacks get a little bit more shadowy!

3,000 Gold

WARP SPEED Enemies will feel the sharp end of your horn!

Path 2: Prince of Darkness Make foes afraid of the Dark

1,700 Gold

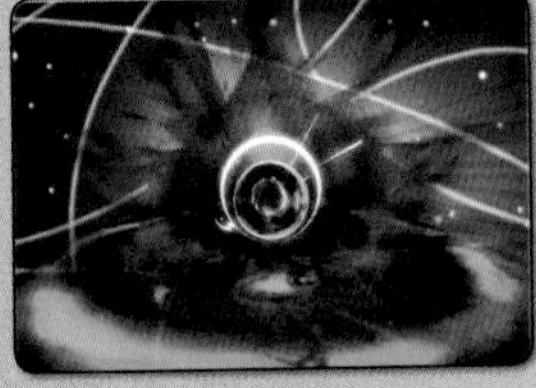

DARK ENERGY CLOUDS Shadow Orbs explode into deadly Dark Energy.

2,200 Gold

UNDER THE COVER OF DARKNESS Dark Energy Clouds protect you from harm.

3,000 Gold

CLOUD GRAVITY Enemies get dragged into Dark Energy Clouds.

LIGHT

SPOTLIGHT

"TIME TO SHINE!"

I discovered Spotlight in the Prismatic Palace, where she astounded me with her magnificent glowing Light. She guarded the Core of Light until Kaos destroyed it and she vanished forever . . . or so I thought!

SOUL GEM
in Soda Springs

LIGHT DRAGONS Shooting Heavenly Auras creates attacking Light Dragons.

STARTING STATS

Max Health	270
Armor	36
Speed	60
Critical Hit	20
Elemental Power	25

PERSONALITY FILE

A bright disposition
Clear-thinking
Respectful
Light on her feet

Starting Powers

Attack 1

EYE BEAMS Blast beams of blinding light from your eyes.

Attack 2

HALO RINGS Say hello to Halo Rings. They refract your light beams.

Power Upgrades

500 Gold

BRIGHT EYES Pass the sunglasses. Those Eye Beams just got brighter.

900 Gold

THE HALO EFFECT Enemies slow down after being hit by a Halo Ring.

700 Gold

HEAVENLY AURA Enemies caught in your light suffer the consequences.

1,200 Gold

HELLO HALOS Send in the ringers with more Halos at once.

"Choose Your Path" Upgrades

Path 1: Visionary Look! Excellent Eye Beams!

1,700 Gold

AURA CHARGE Heavenly Auras are boosted by an Eye Beam blast.

2,200 Gold

LIGHT IT UP Eye Beams make even lighter work of your enemies.

3,000 Gold

BLING Shoot twice the amount of Halo Rings

Path 2: The Ringer Polish your halos!

1,700 Gold

HEAVY HALO Huge Halos cause more havoc.

2,200 Gold

RING SHOT Halo Rings can now shoot light beams on their own!

3,000 Gold

UPLIFTING EXPERIENCE Send foes trapped in Halo Rings into the heavens.

MEET THE SKYLANDER MINIS

These spirited Sidekicks have helped the Skylanders on many a mission. Now, they've all joined Skylanders Academy to learn how to be the best that they can be—and how to take down Kaos and the Doom Raiders!

MINI JINI	
Maximum Health	410
Speed	85
Armor	48
Critical Hit	80
Elemental Power	25

SPRY	
Maximum Health	280
Speed	70
Armor	18
Critical Hit	30
Elemental Power	25

GILL RUNT	
Maximum Health	270
Speed	50
Armor	6
Critical Hit	50
Elemental Power	25

THUMPLING	
Maximum Health	460
Speed	40
Armor	30
Critical Hit	50
Elemental Power	25

SMALL FRY	
Maximum Health	330
Speed	60
Armor	6
Critical Hit	20
Elemental Power	25

WEERUPTOR	
Maximum Health	290
Speed	50
Armor	18
Critical Hit	30
Elemental Power	25

DROBIT	
Maximum Health	290
Speed	60
Armor	24
Critical Hit	20
Elemental Power	25

TRIGGER SNAPPY	
Maximum Health	200
Speed	70
Armor	30
Critical Hit	50
Elemental Power	25

TERRABITE

Maximum Health	310
Speed	50
Armor	18
Critical Hit	30
Elemental Power	25

BOP

Maximum Health	310
Speed	50
Armor	12
Critical Hit	20
Elemental Power	25

EYE SMALL

Maximum Health	430
Speed	50
Armor	30
Critical Hit	50
Elemental Power	25

HIJINX

Maximum Health	270
Speed	60
Armor	18
Critical Hit	30
Elemental Power	25

PET VAC

Maximum Health	240
Speed	70
Armor	12
Critical Hit	20
Elemental Power	25

BREEZE

Maximum Health	270
Speed	70
Armor	18
Critical Hit	50
Elemental Power	25

BARKLEY

Maximum Health	430
Speed	40
Armor	24
Critical Hit	40
Elemental Power	25

WHISPER ELF

Maximum Health	270
Speed	70
Armor	12
Critical Hit	50
Elemental Power	25

KNOW YOUR ENEMY

DOOM RAIDERS

They're the worst of the worst—no wonder Kaos wanted to team up with them! Once you've trapped them, send them on a Villain Quest to help them redeem themselves for all their evil deeds.

GULPER

His gulp is worse than his bite!

TRAP WITH: Water Trap

CAPTURE IN: Soda Springs

ATTACKS: This greedy slug gets to the point with his trident, but make sure he doesn't gobble you up!

VILLAIN QUEST: Balloon Redemption in Know-It-All Island

The Gulper needs to make amends for ruining Soda Fest, the big blue bully!

HINT

There are a lot of unhappy kids. Give out balloons to cheer them all up!

CHOMPY MAGE

The Champ of Chomp!

TRAP WITH: Life Trap

CAPTURE IN: Chompy Mountain

ATTACKS: When he's not transforming himself into a giant Chompy, he's summoning Chompies to do his bidding!

VILLAIN QUEST: Free the Chompies in Chef Zeppelin

Pepper Jack has Chompies tied up on his kitchen blimp. Have the Chompy Mage set them free!

CHEF PEPPER JACK

For those who like their bad guys extra spicy!

TRAP WITH: Fire Trap

CAPTURE IN: Chef Zeppelin

ATTACKS: Peppers enemies with flaming chilies or charges forward with whirling whisks. Either way, it's a recipe for disaster.

VILLAIN QUEST: Head of the Cheese in Rainfish Riveria

Gather stinky cheese from a tropical ruin. Sound easy? Well it would be if it weren't for the evil giant head.

HINT

The head awakes when you swipe his cheese. Don't let him touch you!

DREAMCATCHER

You don't want this head in your head

TRAP WITH: Air Trap

CAPTURE IN: Telescope Towers

ATTACKS: Whips up tornadoes that will leave you tossing in your sleep. And her dream snatchers are simply nightmarish!

VILLAIN QUEST: Sweet Dreams in Wilikin Workshop

Rochester can't get to sleep. Dreamcatcher should be able to help with that!

DR. KRANKCASE

Not the healing kind of doctor!

TRAP WITH: Tech Trap

CAPTURE IN: Wilikin Workshop

ATTACKS: Those spider legs can be sent a-spinning, and his goo gun ensures enemies come to a sticky end!

VILLAIN QUEST: Diorama Drama in Time Town

The Wilikin wants to show the Doctor a diorama. Let's hope he doesn't goo-gun the show. He'll do anything for a new hat!

WOLFGANG

His music is edgy—sharp-steel edgy!

TRAP WITH: Undead Trap

CAPTURE IN: The Future of Skylands

ATTACKS: A swipe of his guitar strikes more than a chord for Wolfgang's foe, and his slide can bring enemies to their knees!

VILLAIN QUEST: An Inconvenience of Imps in The Future of Skylands

Lockmaster Imps are running wild. Lure them to the vacuum droid with Wolfgang's music.

HINT

Destroy the mysterious blue powder to attract the imps' attention.

THE GOLDEN QUEEN

As good as gold and a lot more evil!

TRAP WITH: Earth Trap

CAPTURE IN: Lair of the Golden Queen

ATTACKS: Traps enemies in gold and then swipes at them with her golden staff. That'll take the shine off anyone!

VILLAIN QUEST: Bank On This! in The Ultimate Weapon

Dr. Noobry's Piggybank-o-matic 3001 isn't working. He needs The Golden Queen to make the little piggy snort treasure.

KAOS

Needs no introduction.

TRAP WITH: Kaos Trap

CAPTURE IN: The Ultimate Weapon

ATTACKS: This ultra-Villain has a whole slew of devastating elemental attacks, plus he can shoot lasers from his eyes. Watch out!

VILLAIN QUEST: Who Wants Kaos Kake? in Skylanders Academy

Blobbers needs a little help from Kaos to win the Bake-Off with a magnificent Kaos Kake.

LIGHT AND DARK SUPER VILLAINS

LUMINOUS

He's got real star power. From an actual star!

TRAP WITH: Light Trap

CAPTURE IN: Sunscraper Spire

ATTACKS: He fires illuminating laser blasts of light and uses crystal shards to defeat enemies.

VILLAIN QUEST: Buzz Has a Hat? in Sunscraper Spire

Buzz needs to get his lucky hat back! Send Luminous to retrieve it.

NIGHTSHADE

He'll steal the show. And everything else!

TRAP WITH: Dark Trap

CAPTURE IN: Midnight Museum

ATTACKS: This master thief punches enemies and pull coins from their pockets, throws a cannonball to stun them, and can turn invisible, too.

VILLAIN QUEST: Crown Without a King in Midnight Museum

Deactivate the security system to collect the King of Woodburrow's crown.

ROGUES GALLERY

It wasn't just the Doom Raiders who escaped Cloudcracker Prison. Can you round up these dastardly ne'er-do-wells, too?

RAGE MAGE

He's all the Rage!

TRAP WITH: Magic Trap

CAPTURE IN: Secret Sewers of Supreme Stink

ATTACKS: A strike from Rage Mage's staff drives enemies into a frenzy, while his floating ball of fury is enough to make anyone angry!

VILLAIN QUEST: Ice Cream in the Future in The Future of Skylands

Noobman's ice-cream business is failing, and his assets are frozen. He needs Rage Mage's advertising skills. No, seriously!

BOMB SHELL

Did you hear the one about the tortoise and the bomb?

TRAP WITH: Magic Trap

CAPTURE IN: Chef Zeppelin

ATTACKS: Bomb Shell loves going into a shelly spin, and if that doesn't work, he lobs the odd bomb–or seven!

VILLAIN QUEST: Construction Destruction in Mystic Mill

The trolls are building a fort. Grab the explosives and put them in place to bring the troll's base tumbling down.

HINT

There's more dynamite than you need, so why not stockpile as you explore?

PAIN-YATTA

HINT

Protect the Geckos from attack as they sing.

Filled with candy. And evil.

TRAP WITH: Magic Trap

CAPTURE IN: Telescope Towers

ATTACK: There's nothing sweet about Pain-Yatta's lollipop sucker-slam, and his candy leaves a sour taste in your mouth!

VILLAIN QUEST: I'm with the Band in Secret Sewers of Supreme Stink

Bag O' Bones needs Pain-Yatta to get his Gecko Chorus's single to the Capybara King.

SCRAP SHOOTER

One creature's trash is another one's treasure!

TRAP WITH: Fire Trap

CAPTURE IN: Wilikin Workshop

ATTACKS: It's a real face-off when Scrap Shooter blasts into action. And that's even before he rolls out the explosive barrels!

VILLAIN QUEST: Pirates of the Broken Table in Wilikin Workshop

Yoho wants to play Skystones Smash, but the pesky pirates have smashed their own table. They need Scrap Shooter to rebuild it.

GRINNADE

A walking time bomb. Literally!

TRAP WITH: Fire Trap

CAPTURE IN: Operation: Troll Rocket Steal

ATTACKS: When he's not blowing his own top, this explosive fellow is leading a bunch of bombing clones into battle.

VILLAIN QUEST: Miner Troubles 2 in Skyhighlands

Diggs has miners buried underground and needs Grinnade to blow them back to the surface.

SMOKE SCREAM

No one ever told him not to play with fire!

TRAP WITH: Fire Trap

CAPTURE IN: The Ultimate Weapon

ATTACKS: If this troll's flamethrower doesn't burn up the room, his barrel bombs certainly will!

VILLAIN QUEST: Fight Doom With Boom in The Ultimate Weapon

Buzz needs help blasting a barrier aside so he can get to his circuit breaker. "Boomsticks!" as I believe the security chief would say!

TUSSLE SPROUT

Even more dangerous than a Brussels sprout.

TRAP WITH: Earth Trap

CAPTURE IN: Know-It-All Island

ATTACKS: This little stinker leaves a nasty stink in the nostrils, especially with all those smelly seeds. Yuck!

VILLAIN QUEST: Sproutin' Up in The Phoenix Psantuary

A simple one. All Tussle Sprout has to do is plant himself to create a bridge. Villainous treasure awaits!

GRAVE CLOBBER

A face only a mummy could love!

TRAP WITH: Earth Trap

CAPTURE IN: The Golden Desert

ATTACKS: A swipe of those hands will leave you stiff. This mummy's bony defenses bring grave consequences, too!

VILLAIN QUEST: Where is Flynn in Lair of the Golden Queen

Flynn has been captured by the Golden Queen and locked in a labyrinth. Find the three buttons to lower the defenses.

HINT

Don't worry about fighting enemies if you can get past them. You'll just be wasting time!

CHOMP CHEST

Who better to find treasure than a chest . . . with teeth!

TRAP WITH: Earth Trap

CAPTURE IN: Monster Marsh

ATTACK: Chomp Chest's chompers give Chompies a run for their money, and his enemies will rush to wherever he marks with an X.

VILLAIN QUEST: Hot Diggity Dash in Secret Sewers of Supreme Stink

Eat as many hot dogs as possible before dinnertime runs out. What a shame enemies are out to give you indigestion.

HINT

Chomp a hamburger to get extra time.

BONE CHOMPY

Even skeleton Chompies gotta eat!

TRAP WITH: Undead Trap

CAPTURE IN: The Golden Desert

ATTACKS: If you think Bone Chompy can give a nasty nip, wait until you feel his jaw-traps snap together! Ouch!

VILLAIN QUEST: Paging Dr. Bone Chompy in Operation: Troll Rocket Steal

Curious as it may seem, Bone Chompy has healing powers. Once the challenge is completed, he'll be able to treat injured Mabu soldiers.

HOOD SICKLE

Blink and you'll miss him. But he won't miss you.

TRAP WITH: Undead Trap

CAPTURE IN: Telescope Towers

ATTACKS: Teleporting summons ghosts from beyond, but swinging Hood's Sickle busts them again–and enemies, too!

VILLAIN QUEST: Hatastrophy in Hatterson's Hat Store at Skylanders Academy

Trolls are manufacturing fake hats. Destroy their knock-off kilns so Hatterson can open for business.

HINT

Hood Sickle's scythe makes short work of those counterfeiting machines.

MASKER MIND

Everyone's entitled to HIS opinion!

TRAP WITH: Undead Trap

CAPTURE IN: Rainfish Riviera

ATTACK: A single mental blast will blow your mind–and the rest of you, too, for that matter.

VILLAIN QUEST: Hypnosis Schnipnosis in Telescope Towers

A Mabu scientist believes Hypnosis is impossible. Change his mind, will you?

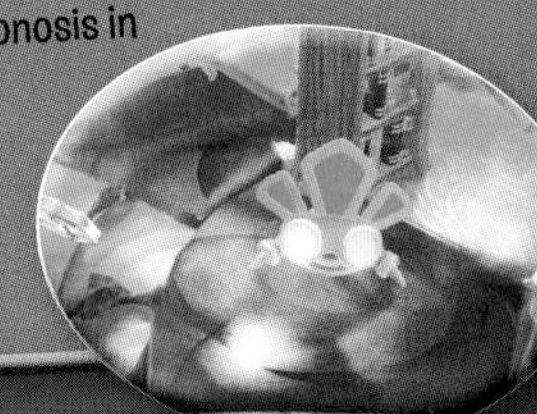

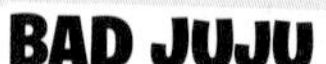

BAD JUJU

She'll take you for a spin!

TRAP WITH: Air Trap

CAPTURE IN: Lair of the Golden Queen

ATTACKS: Twisting tornadoes and lightning bolts from above! Stormy weather lies ahead!

VILLAIN QUEST: Remote Location in Lair of the Golden Queen

Glumshanks needs to dig down deep, and only Bad Juju's tornadoes will do!

BUZZER BEAK

See what the buzz is all about!

TRAP WITH: Air Trap

CAPTURED IN: KNOW-IT-ALL ISLAND

ATTACKS: This whirly-bird sends his blades spinning or body-slams from on high!

VILLAIN QUEST: Family Reunion in The Phoenix Psanctuary

The Copter Birds want to welcome their criminal cousin back into the flock. How sweet!

KRANKENSTEIN

So strong, he fears nothing . . . except termites!

TRAP WITH: Air Trap

CAPTURE IN: Mystic Mill

ATTACKS: Getting drawn into Krankenstein's vacuum arm simply sucks! Sucks! Ha-ha, that's a good one. I must tell Hugo . . .

VILLAIN QUEST: Onward Wilikin Soldiers in Operation: Troll Rocket Steal

Teach Wooster how to build an army of Wilikin warriors!

BROCCOLI GUY

Heals his friends, hurts his enemies!

TRAP WITH: Life Trap

CAPTURE IN: Chompy Mountain

ATTACKS: Turns out Broccoli is bad for you–if you're a foe, that is. If you're a friend, then this green mage can conjure up health-giving food!

VILLAIN QUEST: Broccoli Guy En Fuego in Chef Zeppelin

Bernie needs Broccoli Guy's help in the Kitchen of Shame to prove to the other chefs that he can cook a great meal that isn't on fire.

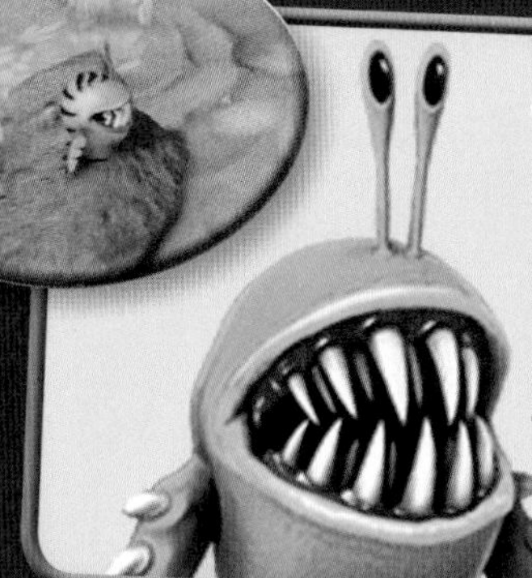

CHOMPY

The classic Skylands Chompy!

TRAP WITH: Life Trap

CAPTURE IN: Mirror of Mystery

ATTACKS: Chompy does exactly what his name says he would: He Chomps! He can also summon a gang of mini Chompies that follow him around and attack enemies.

VILLAIN QUEST: Workers' Chompensation in Mirror of Mystery

Butterfly needs the Chompy's help to wake up a lazy troll and get him back to work.

CUCKOO CLOCKER

He's cuckoo for clobbering!

TRAP WITH: Life Trap

CAPTURE IN: The Phoenix Psanctuary

ATTACKS: If you think Cuckoo Clocker's voice can leave you stunned, wait until you feel his fists!

VILLAIN QUEST: Song Bird in The Phoenix Psanctuary

A clueless choir needs Cuckoo Clocker's beautiful baritone to add a little harmony to their chorus.

SHEEP CREEP

He's baaaaad news!

TRAP WITH: Life Trap

CAPTURE IN: Soda Springs

ATTACKS: The black sheep in the family's cannons will fleece any foe, and his wool attack will leave "ewe" reeling!

VILLAIN QUEST: Mildly Irritated Sheep in Chompy Mountain

Catapult yourself toward the buffalo battlements to free sheep from troll slavery.

HINT

Target the bottom of the towers and forts to bring the entire thing toppling down.

SHIELD SHREDDER

The best defense is a good offense!

TRAP WITH: Life Trap

CAPTURE IN: Mystic Mill

ATTACKS: What do you prefer? A spinning shield dash or giant buzz-saw blades? Both will leave enemies feeling a little cut-up!

VILLAIN QUEST: Wood-be Band in Wilikin Workshop

Believe it or not, Shield Shredder is just what Gilmour's Wilikin band needs to make marvelous music. Spin those tunes!

BRUISER CRUISER

Give him a big hand. Or two!

TRAP WITH: Tech Trap

CAPTURE IN: Chompy Mountain

ATTACKS: This Troll Walker packs quite a punch–and when he blows his top, he takes enemies with him.

VILLAIN QUEST: Need More Than Singing in Chompy Mountain

Molekin Miners are trapped, but Bruiser Cruiser can blast them free.

SHREDNAUGHT

2 Trolls, 1 giant chainsaw, unlimited possibilities.

TRAP WITH: Tech Trap

CAPTURE IN: The Phoenix Psanctuary

ATTACKS: Troll one and Troll two are the very definition of double trouble, thanks to their giant chainsaw.

VILLAIN QUEST: Sure Beats Keys in Mystic Mill

Loggins needs Shrednaught to saw through a hardwood barrier! The saw loser becomes a saw winner!

BRAWLRUS

Brawl + Walrus = Brawlrus!

TRAP WITH: Tech Trap

CAPTURE IN: Rainfish Riviera

ATTACKS: Shoots spinning starfish from his barnacled bazooka! Some bigger than others!

VILLAIN QUEST: Submarine Bros 4 Life in Rainfish Riviera

Argle Bargle's submarine is sinking, but he will only open up to his old buddy Brawlrus!

TROLLING THUNDER

Wears a tank for pants!

TRAP WITH: Tech Trap

CAPTURE IN: The Nightmare Express

ATTACKS: He shoots shells from his turret, and can also backfire to cause more damage to nearby enemies.

VILLAIN QUEST: Statue of Limitations in The Nightmare Express

Da Pinchy needs Trolling Thunder's help to break a boulder that is blocking his beautiful statue of Captain Flynn.

MAB LOBS

A Mabu gone bad? No way!

TRAP WITH: Tech Trap

CAPTURE IN: Mirror of Mystery

ATTACKS: This bad-news Mabu lobs three large bombs at enemies, or several smaller ones at once.

VILLAIN QUEST: Fishness Protection Program in Mirror of Mystery

Kaos needs Mab Lobs's help to scare away his fishy friend before the village gets attacked.

CHILL BILL

Was evil BEFORE it was cool.

TRAP WITH: Water Trap

CAPTURE IN: The Phoenix Psanctuary

ATTACKS: Chill Bill aims to freeze, that's for sure. Enemies end up cooling their heels in a block of ice!

VILLAIN QUEST: The Cold Front in Chompy Mountain

Troll Radio is not what it was. Send in Chill Bill to DJ the ultimate chill-out!

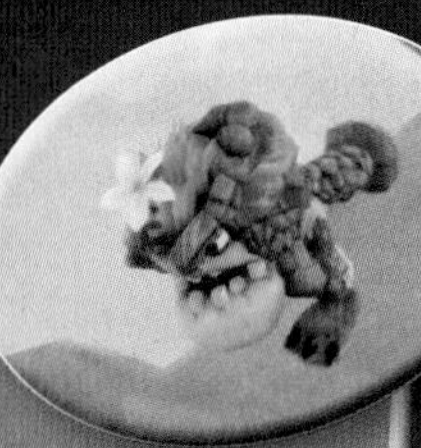

SLOBBER TRAP

Just your average plant monster dog!

TRAP WITH: Water Trap

CAPTURE IN: Know-It-All Island

ATTACKS: Slobber licks his enemies into shape, literally. He's got a pretty vile piledriver move, too.

VILLAIN QUEST: Gumbus's Fortune in Know-It-All Island

Gumbus needs a statue toppling, and Slobber Trap is the dog-thing for the job!

BRAWL AND CHAIN

No chains, No Pain!

TRAP WITH: Water Trap

CAPTURE IN: Rainfish Riviera

ATTACKS: Whip out that hook or take enemies for a spin!

VILLAIN QUEST: Fairy Night Lights in Telescope Towers

Grab lanterns from the tree of light and get them to the Mabu houses as quickly as you can.

THREATPACK

A troll in a jetpack. Now THAT'S a threat!

TRAP WITH: Water Trap

CAPTURE IN: Operation: Troll Rocket Steal

ATTACKS: This former professor barges forward with his water-jetpack. Just make sure you stand behind him!

VILLAIN QUEST: You Break It, You Fix It in Skyhighlands

Tessa needs a cannon repaired. Know any tech-minded trolls that could help?

HINT

Use the bombs to blow any barriers sky-high!

CROSS CROW

Don't cross Cross Crow!

TRAP WITH: Water Trap

CAPTURE IN: Time Town

ATTACKS: Wielding the crossest Crossbow in the history of combat, this birdie berserker can also summon a murder of crows!

VILLAIN QUEST: Skylands' Biggest Fans in Time Town

Trolls have stopped the windmills so the birds of Skylands don't have enough wind to fly. Lower the powerfoils to get those blades whirring.

FISTICUFFS

Speaks softly and carries a big fist!

TRAP WITH: Dark Trap

CAPTURE IN: Secret Sewers of Supreme Stink

ATTACKS: No good backing away from Fisticuffs! He can throw a long punch. Quite literally, in fact!

VILLAIN QUEST: Outhouse Back In-House in Monster Marsh

A Mabu with an, ahem, urgent need needs Fisticuff to drag his outhouse back in. No clowning around now.

TAE KWON CROW

Ninja skills and the fiendishness of a bird.

TRAP WITH: Dark Trap

CAPTURE IN: Skyhighlands

ATTACKS: A blade as sharp as his beak or a fistful of flying feather stars. Follow the dishonorable path!

VILLAIN QUEST: Gopher the Gold in The Golden Desert

Tessa needs your help to protect gophers from the Hazard Birds. She's trying to track down the rarer than rare golden gopher.

HINT

Don't let the Hazard Birds take the gophers to their nests.

EYE SCREAM

We all scream for Eye Scream!

TRAP WITH: Dark Trap

CAPTURE IN: Monster Marsh

ATTACKS: Spits roving eyeballs of various sizes. Disgusting.

VILLAIN QUEST: Paranormal Captivity in Monster Marsh

Cali has a gaggle of ghosts ready to scare away the curse of Monster Marsh. Find where the scaredy spooks are hiding and get them back to their ship.

HINT

Don't get hit when leading ghosts. They'll rush back to where you found them.

LOB GOBLIN

Danger—high voltage!

TRAP WITH: Light Trap

CAPTURE IN: The Nightmare Express

ATTACKS: This goblin throws three exploding electrical mines, or one charged super mine that explodes when enemies come close.

VILLAIN QUEST: Grand Theft Plan in The Nightmare Express

Peebs needs Lob Goblin to help him intercept the secret plans for the trolls' latest tank and gate-locking technology.

BLASTER-TRON

From the future. This means lasers.

TRAP WITH: Light Trap

CAPTURE IN: The Future of Skylands

ATTACKS: Drag enemies to you using Blaster-Tron's tractor beam–and then butt them away again with a turbo boost!

VILLAIN QUEST: Help Diggs Dig in The Golden Desert

Digs needs some help finding his treasure. Blaster-Tron's magnetic personality should do it!

EYE FIVE

I don't recommend playing patty-cake with him.

TRAP WITH: Light Trap

CAPTURE IN: Monster Marsh

ATTACKS: His punches will make your eyes water, and as for his super stare? It's simply shocking!

VILLAIN QUEST: Chongo! in Rainfish Riviera

Doublooney the pirate has invented a crazy new game–Chongo! Simply bash minions and collect treasure!

HINT

Use the weapons that Dreamcatcher drops from the sky. My favorite is the UFO! Out of this world, that one!

MINIONS-A-GO-GO!

It's not just escaped villains you have to fight, Portal Master! The minions of evil are everywhere!

CHOMPIES

Skylands wouldn't be Skylands without Chompies. In fact, it'd probably be a lot nicer. The little biters come in all shapes and sizes. Goo Chompies are a new, particularly nasty breed. They turn into bubbling puddles of poison!

CHOMPY WORMS

And you thought all Chompies were small? These massive beasts burrow through the sand, although rumor has it that they might yet become beautiful butterflies—or ugly ones, at least!

TROLLS

Tech-loving trolls love blowing things up. Or just hitting things, for that matter. Watch out for the new Eggsecutioners. You'll need to crack the shells of these hardboiled trolls to whip them into shape.

OOGLERS

Don't be dazzled by these sprites' giant peepers. You'll never see their energy lines creeping up on you!

EVILIKIN

Remember the Willikin, Kaos's childhood playthings? Well, meet their utterly evil cousins. They'll blow you up as soon as look at you!

CUDDLES

They look cute and just want to give you a hug—one that will crush you, that is!

CYCLOPS DRAGON

This undead mother surrounds herself with her monstrous eyeball babies! Imagine the family portraits!

SNOZZLER

Those huge noses are nothing to sneeze at. Hit them when they're on the ground!

INTO THE ADVENTURE

CHAPTER 1

SODA SPRINGS

The opening of the new Skylanders Academy has been disrupted by escaped Villains from Cloudcracker Prison. How is that even possible? Learn how to use your Skylanders by bringing the first fugitives to justice!

Goals

- ◯ Find and defeat Sheep Creep
- ◯ Save Soda Springs from disaster

Dares

- ◯ No lives lost
- ◯ Find all 17 areas
- ◯ Defeat 30 enemies
- ◯ Defeat 2 Villains
- ◯ Open 4 *Traptanium* Gates

Difficult Dares

- ◯ Time to beat: 11:30
- ◯ Don't switch

Items

- ◯ 1 Story Scroll
- ◯ 4 Treasure Chests
- ◯ 3 Soul Gems
- ◯ 1 Winged Sapphire
- ◯ 1 Legendary Treasure
- ◯ 4 Hats

Areas

- ◯ Sugar Plateau
- ◯ Cola Stream
- ◯ Backwash Spillway
- ◯ Soda Flats
- ◯ Hidden Flavor Grotto
- ◯ Natural Ingredients Tree
- ◯ Seltzer Pit
- ◯ Carbonated Plant-Water
- ◯ Twisting Top
- ◯ Secret Ingredients
- ◯ Melon Flavor Farm-Life
- ◯ Sugar-Free Landing
- ◯ Zero Calorie Cavern-Tech
- ◯ Really Secret Spot
- ◯ Grape-Flavored Vista
- ◯ Bottleneck Balcony
- ◯ Fizzleworts Rooftop

Sugar Plateau

Test your weapons by clearing the path of debris. You never know what you'll find.

HINT: *Use the soda cannon to blast through walls. "Sweet," as Tessa would say.*

EON'S TIP

Changing the music on a troll radio set can sometimes release extra coins!

Cola Stream

After you've pushed around some turtles, splash into the Cola Stream to jump down to hidden treasure.

HINT: *Use the jump pad to bounce back up to Sugar Plateau.*

Soda Flats

It's time to capture your first Villain, Portal Master. Defeat Sheep Creep and then trap him in the Life Trap.

HINT: *Before plugging a gap with a turtle, continue around to find a precious grotto.*

Natural Ingredients Tree

Defeat all of the Chompies in the Arena to open the Battle Gate. This should be an easy win, Portal Master.

HINT: *Use a Trap Master to smash the* Traptanium *to earn yourself some extra treasure.*

Carbonated Plant

Use a Water Trap Master to open the *Traptanium* Gate. Make sure you leap on that bounce pad before you rush on.

HINT: *Push the turtle into the airflow to get around to your first Hat. How dashing!*

Twisting Top

Leap off a cliff to find an illuminating *Traptanium* Gate. Use a Light Trap Master and take advantage of the Soda Cannon to get through the doors and collect a Hat and a Soul Gem.

HINT: *Want two Soul Gems for the price of one? Then use the bounce pad down below.*

EON'S TIP

A weighty problem awaits in Melon Flavor Farm. Can you tip the scales in your favor?

Sugar-Free Landing

Defeat the Chompies, but head down to the *Traptanium* Gate before charging through the Battle Gate.

HINT: *There's a really secret spot down below if you dare to take a jump!*

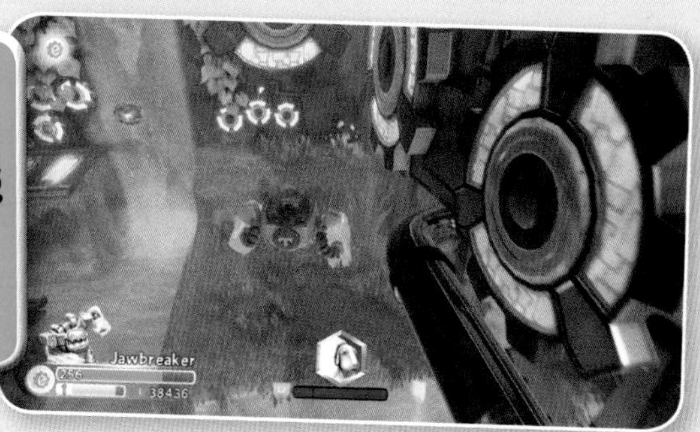

Grape-Flavored Vista

Watch out for flying barrels. The Gulper doesn't care whom he hits when he's thirsty!

HINT: *Bounce over to the soda cauldron and smash it before the Gulper quenches his thirst.*

EXTRA

Used a captured Villain to open a Villain stash for extra treasure!

Bottleneck Balcony

You need to hop across the cork stepping-stones before the Gulper belches them out of place!

HINT: *Defeat the Gulper by swapping his favorite soda for disgusting bottom-feeding suction-eel flavor. Nasty!*

CHAPTER 2

KNOW-IT-ALL ISLAND

The Knuckleheads of Know-It-All-Island know everything there is to know about the Doom Raiders. Let Buzz lead you on an information-gathering expedition!

Goals

- ◯ Gather info about the Doom Raiders
- ◯ Clear out trolls from the island

Dares

- ◯ No lives lost
- ◯ Find all 11 areas
- ◯ Defeat 45 enemies
- ◯ Defeat 3 Villains
- ◯ Open 3 *Traptanium* Gates

Difficult Dares

- ◯ Time to beat: 9:20
- ◯ Don't switch
- ◯ Complete 2 Villain Quests

Items

- ◯ 1 Story Scroll
- ◯ 4 Treasure Chests
- ◯ 2 Soul Gems
- ◯ 1 Winged Sapphire
- ◯ 1 Legendary Treasure
- ◯ 3 Hats

Areas

- ◯ Pompous Point-Life
- ◯ Told-You-So Terrace
- ◯ Stuck-Up Steppes
- ◯ The Weighting Room
- ◯ Windbag Woods-Air
- ◯ Enchanted Forest-Life
- ◯ Steam Vent Junction
- ◯ Boulder Falls Circle
- ◯ Shadowy Sanctum-Dark
- ◯ Patronizing Plateau-Life
- ◯ Bragger's Retreat

Pompous Point

Before grabbing the key and unlocking the door, take the Gulper to meet Mags to make amends.

HINT: *Smashing the* ***Traptanium*** *Crystals will lead you straight into a Tussle Sprout ambush.*

Stuck-Up Steppes

After gaining useful information about the Chompy Mage from the first Knucklehead, head over to the Elemental Gate.

HINT: *Throw boulders into the pit to raise the islands so you can grab a Hat worthy of a detective.*

Windbag Woods

After opening the double-locked Gate, you'll face a terrifying troll tank.

HINT: *Use a Life Trap Master to open the Elemental Gate and blow up Troll Lumberjack machines.*

Steam Vent Junction

Before following Blobbers up the Steam Vent, head to the left and smash those **Traptanium** Crystals to find another escaped Villain.

HINT: *You'll come across the first boulder puzzle next. Unplug the vents by rolling the boulders over the hissing steam.*

EXTRA

Guide the sphere in Shadowy Sanctum into its home to release a ship-faring cap.

Bragger's Retreat

Shut Slobber Trap's trap and then take the Villain back to Gumbus for his Villain Quest.

HINT: *Send the Trolls packing by blasting their fiendish flying machines out of the sky. Just aim for the pilots.*

CHAPTER 3

CHOMPY MOUNTAIN

The Chompy Mage is loose on Chompy Mountain. Well, it is his home. Bring him to justice, Portal Master, and his little hand puppet, too!

Goals
- ◯ Gather Mabu Workers
- ◯ Unlock Chompy Mountain Entrance
- ◯ Find and defeat the Chompy Mage

Dares
- ◯ No lives lost
- ◯ Find all 20 areas
- ◯ Defeat 110 enemies
- ◯ Defeat 3 Villains
- ◯ Open 2 *Traptanium* Gates

Difficult Dares
- ◯ Time to beat: 20:30
- ◯ Don't switch
- ◯ Complete 3 Villain Quests

Items
- ◯ 1 Story Scroll
- ◯ 4 Treasure Chests
- ◯ 3 Soul Gems
- ◯ 1 Winged Sapphire
- ◯ 1 Legendary Treasure
- ◯ 3 Hats

Areas
- ◯ Mabu Landing Pier
- ◯ Old Mabu Town
- ◯ Snuckle's House
- ◯ Rizzo's House
- ◯ Crystal Caves-Magic
- ◯ Nort's House
- ◯ Wishing Well
- ◯ Spinner's Landing-Life
- ◯ Overgrown Rampart-Tech
- ◯ Mountain Falls Lagoon
- ◯ Troll Fortress-Villains
- ◯ K-TROLL Troll Radio
- ◯ Chompy Mountain
- ◯ Rizzo's Rescue-Magic
- ◯ Artillery Storage
- ◯ Undead Vista-Undead
- ◯ Nort's Rescue-Life
- ◯ Chompy Hatchery
- ◯ Snuckle's Rescue-Villains
- ◯ Chompy Head Spire

Old Mabu Town

Buzz has scared away all the Mabu workers. Round them up and get them to work.

HINT: *Have a look around Rizzo's House after you've rescued him. What you'll find is truly Magic.*

EXTRA

Use a bomb from Rizzo's House to blow up the wishing well and take a dip!

Spinner's Landing

After defeating the trolls, screw down the Chompy coil to start unlocking the door to the mountain.

HINT: *The Chompy Mage will attack after you cross the bridge. Shove his own cannons in place to blast the wicked wizard.*

Overgrown Rampart

Bruiser Cruiser is waiting for you over the new bridge. The tricky troll is most vulnerable when he's rebuilding himself.

HINT: *Once you've trapped Bruiser Cruiser, head to the left for a miner challenge.*

EON'S TIP

Look for some perfectly camouflaged crystals in Mountain Falls Lagoon.

Chompy Mountain

After opening the gate to the mountain, you'll need to rescue the Mabu Defense Force. Blast open a gate to bust out Rizzo.

HINT: *Once you've learned how to play Skystones Smash, you may want to revisit this area, Portal Master.*

Chompy Head Spire

It's time to face the Chompy Mage. First he'll send in his Chompy hordes. Annoying, but easy to defeat.

HINT: *The Chompy Mage's Magma Form is trickier. Jump over those fire rings before you feel their burn.*

CHAPTER 4

THE PHOENIX PSANCTUARY

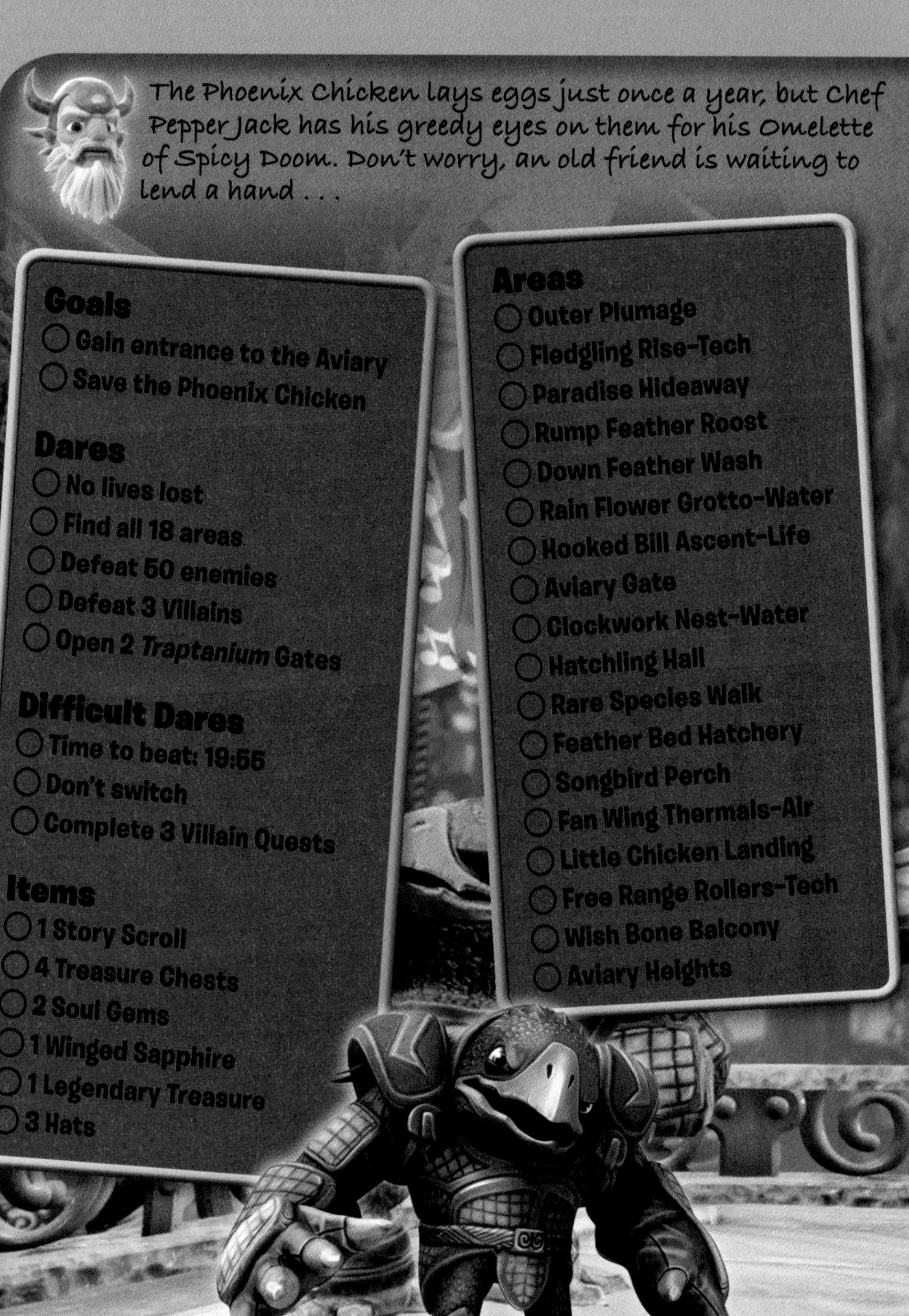

The Phoenix Chicken lays eggs just once a year, but Chef Pepper Jack has his greedy eyes on them for his Omelette of Spicy Doom. Don't worry, an old friend is waiting to lend a hand . . .

Goals

- ◯ Gain entrance to the Aviary
- ◯ Save the Phoenix Chicken

Dares

- ◯ No lives lost
- ◯ Find all 18 areas
- ◯ Defeat 50 enemies
- ◯ Defeat 3 Villains
- ◯ Open 2 *Traptanium* Gates

Difficult Dares

- ◯ Time to beat: 19:55
- ◯ Don't switch
- ◯ Complete 3 Villain Quests

Items

- ◯ 1 Story Scroll
- ◯ 4 Treasure Chests
- ◯ 2 Soul Gems
- ◯ 1 Winged Sapphire
- ◯ 1 Legendary Treasure
- ◯ 3 Hats

Areas

- ◯ Outer Plumage
- ◯ Fledgling Rise-Tech
- ◯ Paradise Hideaway
- ◯ Rump Feather Roost
- ◯ Down Feather Wash
- ◯ Rain Flower Grotto-Water
- ◯ Hooked Bill Ascent-Life
- ◯ Aviary Gate
- ◯ Clockwork Nest-Water
- ◯ Hatchling Hall
- ◯ Rare Species Walk
- ◯ Feather Bed Hatchery
- ◯ Songbird Perch
- ◯ Fan Wing Thermals-Air
- ◯ Little Chicken Landing
- ◯ Free Range Rollers-Tech
- ◯ Wish Bone Balcony
- ◯ Aviary Heights

Outer Plumage

Drop a Boingo Nut into holes in the ground to grow vine bridges. Watch out, because the Eggsecutioners will soon scramble!

HINT: *After crossing to Fledgling Rise, throw the lever to reveal a bounce pad!*

EXTRA

Can't jump up to a cage containing treasure? Then try jumping down to it instead!

Hooked Bill Ascent

The Blocker Birds live up to their name, until you feed these feathered nuts a nut!

HINT: *You'll need to fight an army of trolls to get the key to the Psanctuary. Try taking out the grappling hooks as they arrive.*

Fan Wing Thermals

Breezing through the Air Element Gate, ride the thermals to take to the skies. And if you can't quite reach a platform then jump to it!

HINT: *After you're done, head to the right for a special Songbird challenge.*

Free Range Rollers

Try to dodge the eggs rolling down the Aviary. Don't worry, you can always smash them before they smash you!

HINT: *Check out the landing to the right, halfway up. Once you've dealt with the Eggsecutioners, make sure you wish for treasure.*

Aviary Heights

The heat is on in Chef Pepper Jack's arena. Jump on the Phoenix Chicks when they appear for extra protection.

HINT: *Keep chomping all the food you can find, because Cuckoo Clocker is waiting in round three!*

CHAPTER 5

CHEF ZEPPELIN

Pepper Jack has taken one of the eggs and can now make his bomb! Flynn will take you to his blimp-based kitchens to serve Skylander justice!

Goals
- ◯ Clear out the troll defenses
- ◯ Find and defeat Chef Pepper Jack

Dares
- ◯ No lives lost
- ◯ Find all 19 areas
- ◯ Defeat 50 enemies
- ◯ Defeat 2 Villains
- ◯ Open 3 *Traptanium* Gates

Difficult Dares
- ◯ Time to beat: 19:55
- ◯ Don't switch
- ◯ Complete 2 Villain Quests

Items
- ◯ 1 Story Scroll
- ◯ 4 Treasure Chests
- ◯ 1 Soul Gem
- ◯ 1 Winged Sapphire
- ◯ 1 Legendary Treasure
- ◯ 3 Hats

Areas
- ◯ Landing Pan
- ◯ Main Counter Top-Fire
- ◯ Side Spinner
- ◯ Bottom Shelf
- ◯ Peculiarity of Light-Light
- ◯ Tail Winds-Air
- ◯ Main Kabobs
- ◯ Chopping Block
- ◯ Kitchen of Shame
- ◯ Topside Burners
- ◯ Smorgasbord-Villains
- ◯ Top Shelf
- ◯ Cheese Graters
- ◯ Port Gangway
- ◯ Auxiliary Kitchen
- ◯ Cooling Rack-Magic
- ◯ Command Kitchen
- ◯ Oven-Fire
- ◯ Garbage Disposal
- ◯ Boss Fight Arena

Turret Sequence

Pepper Jack's Zeppelin has heavy air defenses. Shoot down the Troll flying machines, but watch out for greenskins wearing copter-packs!

HINT: *Once the air defenses are taken care of, turn your attention to the cannons. Oh, and watch out for gems, too!*

Main Counter Top

Use the levers to align the cannons and take down barriers ahead. Then check out the deck to the right for not one, but two Elemental Gates.

HINT: *To continue, leap over the flaming Kabobs to the left, but keep an eye out for a Soul Gem.*

EXTRA

Leap down a deck for a Legendary Treasure, but be warned: You'll have to face the Kabobs again!

Cooling Rack

Take out the trolls to lure Bomb Shell out of his, well, shell! Once he's trapped, you'll be able to grab a special key!

HINT: *Need a bomb? Then keep your eyes peeled as you race down to unlock the door!*

Command Kitchen

Learn how to play Skystones Smash from Batterson and then take on the Sous Chefs to storm the kitchen!

HINT: *Open the Fire Elemental Gate on the Oven. Then bake bridges by pushing dough over the flames.*

Boss Fight Arena

Pepper Jack's throwing everything he has at you. Leap over the laser lines to stop yourself from sizzling!

HINT: *When the Chef starts to barbeque, jump on the burgers to get off the griddle, but make sure they don't vanish beneath your feet.*

CHAPTER 6

RAINFISH RIVIERA

Mags needs her Information Squid, but it's been captured by pirates in Rainfish Riviera. With Flynn out of action, Cali is angling to take you fishing.

Goals

- ◯ Retrieve Mags's Information Squid

Dares

- ◯ No lives lost
- ◯ Find all 20 areas
- ◯ Defeat 75 enemies
- ◯ Defeat 3 Villains
- ◯ Open 2 *Traptanium* Gates

Difficult Dares

- ◯ Time to beat: 19:30
- ◯ Don't switch
- ◯ Complete 3 Villain Quests

Items

- ◯ 1 Story Scroll
- ◯ 4 Treasure Chests
- ◯ 2 Soul Gems
- ◯ 1 Winged Sapphire
- ◯ 1 Legendary Treasure
- ◯ 3 Hats

Areas

- ◯ Monsoon Point
- ◯ Blowhole Beach-Earth
- ◯ Wastewater Cove
- ◯ Steel Fin Balcony-Undead
- ◯ Fish Bone's Card Shack
- ◯ Brackwater Falls
- ◯ Fish Bone's Retreat-Undead
- ◯ Fish Eyed Walk
- ◯ Fish Eyed Control-Villains
- ◯ Clam Tower
- ◯ Submarine Pen-Water
- ◯ Starfish's Sub
- ◯ Dredger's Yacht-Water
- ◯ Below Deck
- ◯ Dire Sands
- ◯ Barnacle Shoal-Earth
- ◯ Bluster Squall Island-Villains
- ◯ Cheddar House
- ◯ Big Hook
- ◯ Fish Mouth

Blowhole Beach

After defeating Brawlrus and his pirate pack, grab the stack of wood to build a bridge and rejoin Mags.

HINT: *Take the wood from the bridge with you after crossing over. You'll need it again to help open a double-locked Gate.*

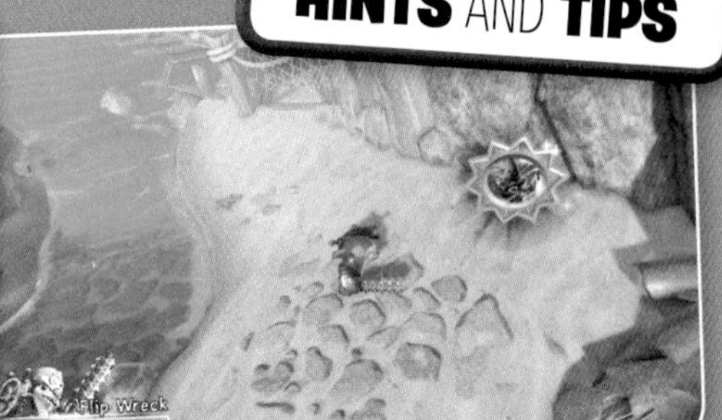

Fish Bone's Card Shack

You'll need to play Skystones Smash to get the other key from Bucko. But beware, an ambush awaits outside the hut.

HINT: *Need a break from battle with Masker Mind? Then leap down for an Undead Gate and a Villain Quest. The Villain will wait!*

Fish Eyed Walk

Nip into Fish Eyed Control to hit the gate control, after defeating a bunch of enemies, of course.

HINT: *Next up you'll use a crane to rebuild the bridge. Better clear the place of pirates first, though.*

EXTRA

Take a leap into the depths at Clam Tower. Brawlrus can help bring in some stylish new headgear.

Barnacle Shoal

Shove the snails around to find a path across the water. You may have to go back on yourself once or twice.

HINT: *Turn left as you come back out of the Elemental Gate for more shell shoving. Do you get the feeling you've done this before?*

Big Hook

The Rainfish has swallowed the Information Squid. Use the crane to grab bait to lure the leviathan near.

HINT: *Once the freaky fish is eating, reel it in with the crane. You'll have to venture into the belly of the beast to find the Squid.*

CHAPTER 7

MONSTER MARSH

Kaos has told Cali that the Dreamcatcher is in the Poisonous Swamp of Bad Decisions, but can we really trust our greatest enemy?

Goals

- ◯ Free Headwick
- ◯ Find Sleepy Village
- ◯ Rescue the Sleepy Villagers

Dares

- ◯ No lives lost
- ◯ Find all 20 areas
- ◯ Defeat 120 enemies
- ◯ Defeat 3 Villains
- ◯ Open 2 *Traptanium* Gates

Difficult Dares

- ◯ Time to beat: 23:45
- ◯ Don't switch
- ◯ Complete 2 Villain Quests

Items

- ◯ 1 Story Scroll
- ◯ 4 Treasure Chests
- ◯ 2 Soul Gems
- ◯ 1 Winged Sapphire
- ◯ 1 Legendary Treasure
- ◯ 4 Hats

Areas

- ◯ Haunted Wreck
- ◯ Haunted Approach
- ◯ Spirestone Mausoleum-Undead
- ◯ Spirestone Graveyard-Villains
- ◯ Spirestone Cliffs
- ◯ Spirestone Grotto
- ◯ Spirestone Crypt-Undead
- ◯ Hungry Isle
- ◯ Windmill Hill
- ◯ Supply Room
- ◯ Secret Basement
- ◯ Little House on the Misty Marsh
- ◯ The Misty Marshes-Villains
- ◯ Dark Hollow-Dark
- ◯ Empty Isle
- ◯ Village Approach-Magic
- ◯ Smuggler's Hideout
- ◯ Sleepy Village
- ◯ Grocer Jack's
- ◯ "Boots" the Cobbler

Haunted Wreck

Head behind Gomper's wrecked ship to shove blocks into a staircase. Now you can grab Krypt King's stormy Soul Gem.

HINT: *Find a gap near the block puzzle to jump down to a treasure-filled grotto.*

Hungry Isle

After rescuing Headwick, take the super-jump pad to Hungry Isle, where Chomp Chest is waiting for you!

HINT: *Jump the flaming barrels as you cross the bridge to the Windmill.*

Little House on the Misty Marsh

Take out all the enemies to open the combat gate. Watch out for those evil little eyes.

HINT: *Solve the lock puzzle to release the fairy Marsha. The Lockmaster Imp will need to keep cool to get past those flames.*

The Misty Marshes

Stay within Marsha's force field to protect yourself from the poisonous swamp.

HINT: *In Dark Hollow, use the pinball flippers to break the barriers and then get all three balls in place to win.*

EXTRA

When on dry land, shove some blocks around to find a Legendary Treasure.

Sleepy Village

Dreamcatcher is stealing the Mabus' dreams. Quick, wake up all the villagers!

HINT: *What a nightmare! Survive Dreamcatcher's arena by watching out for the cracks in the ground.*

CHAPTER 8

TELESCOPE TOWERS

Dreamcatcher is trying to unlock the secrets of **Traptanium** from sleeping Mabu scientists. Headwick will lead you through the weirdest of dreamscapes.

Goals

- ◯ Find and Defeat Dreamcatcher

Dares

- ◯ No lives lost
- ◯ Find all 24 areas
- ◯ Defeat 60 enemies
- ◯ Defeat 3 Villains
- ◯ Open 3 *Traptanium* Gates

Difficult Dares

- ◯ Time to beat: 17:55
- ◯ Don't switch
- ◯ Complete 2 Villain Quests

Items

- ◯ 1 Story Scroll
- ◯ 4 Treasure Chests
- ◯ 2 Soul Gems
- ◯ 1 Winged Sapphire
- ◯ 1 Legendary Treasure
- ◯ 3 Hats

Areas

- ◯ Galactic Bubble Center
- ◯ Pulse Block Plains
- ◯ Embroidered Bridge
- ◯ Chamber Entrance
- ◯ Back-to-Back Stack-N-Jack
- ◯ Watering Hole Encounter-Water
- ◯ Hypnosis Pocus
- ◯ Cosmic Chamber
- ◯ Pulse Block Pillow Pit-Magic
- ◯ Observation Terrace-Enemies
- ◯ Observatory Loggia
- ◯ The Magic Frame Game-Magic
- ◯ Grinding Gears-Tech
- ◯ Meditation Pool
- ◯ Impossible Gravity Collider-Undead
- ◯ Roof Observation Deck-Magic
- ◯ Framing an Art Attack
- ◯ The Great Spiral Observatory-Tech
- ◯ Dream a Little Dream Beds
- ◯ Feng Shui Shove
- ◯ Stairway to the Stars
- ◯ Spiral Balcony
- ◯ Waterfall Fall-Water
- ◯ Library Lock Out

Pulse Block Plains

Jump on the button to release the pulse blocks and then push them into position to reactivate the bridge.

HINT: *When the jack-in-the-boxes on the Embroidered Bridge shake, they're ready to pop!*

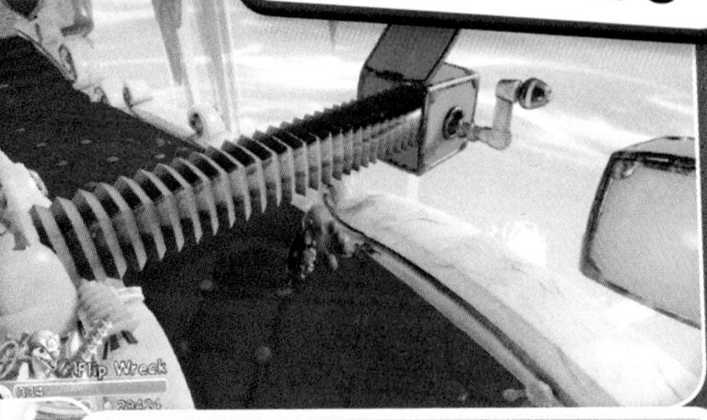

Watering Hole Encounter

You'll need to survive an encounter with Dreamcatcher to pump up the pulse boxes that will lead to the key.

HINT: *Once in the chamber, shake the beds to wake up the snoozing scientists and release more buttons.*

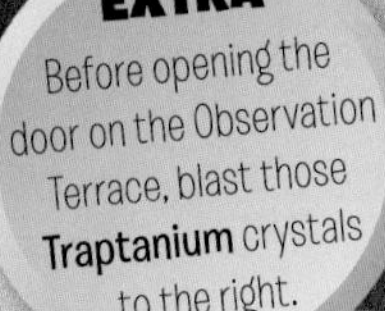

EXTRA

Before opening the door on the Observation Terrace, blast those **Traptanium** crystals to the right.

Impossible Gravity Collider

Be careful, Portal Master, Dreamcatcher sets nightmarish minions against you when you least expect it.

HINT: *After waking the twin Mabu scientists, head to the left for a villainous treat!*

The Great Spiral Observatory

Watch out for surprising jack-in-the-boxes as you make your way to punish Pain-Yatta.

HINT: *Head back to the bottom of the tower to unlock a door to hidden treasure. You might want to jump on that button, too!*

Spiral Balcony

It's time to send Dreamcatcher to sleep. Knock out her force field by unmaking those floating beds.

HINT: *Watch your feet! If a stone flashes red, it's about to disappear.*

CHAPTER 9

MYSTIC MILL

The Doom Raiders are using enchanted wood to create Evilikins. The Mabu Defense Force has been sent to defend the Mystic Mill. What could go wrong?

Goals

- ◯ Regain control of the flagship
- ◯ Take out the Evilikin Turrets
- ◯ Retake the Mill from the Evilikin

Dares

- ◯ No lives lost
- ◯ Find all 19 areas
- ◯ Defeat 55 enemies
- ◯ Defeat 2 Villains
- ◯ Open 2 *Traptanium* Gates

Difficult Dares

- ◯ Time to beat: 12:25
- ◯ Don't switch
- ◯ Complete 2 Villain Quests

Items

- ◯ 1 Story Scroll
- ◯ 4 Treasure Chests
- ◯ 2 Soul Gems
- ◯ 1 Winged Sapphire
- ◯ 1 Legendary Treasure
- ◯ 3 Hats

Areas

- ◯ Mabu Flagship
- ◯ Loading Docks-Earth
- ◯ Lumber Mill Office
- ◯ Wheelhouse A
- ◯ Packing House
- ◯ Mudder's Corner-Villains
- ◯ Wheelhouse B
- ◯ Western Storage Unit-Life
- ◯ Sawdust Processing
- ◯ Waterways
- ◯ Fire Falls-Fire
- ◯ Eastern Storage Unit
- ◯ Power House-Villain
- ◯ Flying Flora-Life
- ◯ Plant Processing . . . Plant
- ◯ Saw Mill Main Gate-Air
- ◯ Nature Bridges-North
- ◯ Nature Bridges-West
- ◯ Pulp Shredder

Mabu Flagship

You need to rescue the Mabu Defense Force. Shove those slippery crates into place to clamber to the ship's wheel.

HINT: *When taking out the gun turrets, concentrate on enemies that can fire on you first! Oh, and shoot any gems you see!*

EXTRA

You'll need a turtle with an explosive personality to collect all the hats in Mystic Mill.

Western Storage Unit

Enter the second hut you come upon to face an escaped Villain who wants to shred you!

HINT: *Once you're in the Waterways, head upstream to find the Fire Elemental Gate.*

Power House

You need two keys to proceed. Using the levers to line up the lasers is a step in the right direction.

HINT: *The second key is up the Waterways. Leap over the logs as you climb.*

Flying Flora

You'll find a *Traptanium* Gate just to the right of the Power House. Jump on the air balloons to find extra riches.

HINT: *Grow a Boingo bridge to slip down the Plant Processing Chimney for the last Hatbox of this chapter.*

Saw Mill Main Gate

After you storm the battle gate, keep straight ahead to build some legendary bridges.

HINT: *After you have your treasure, head back to the Pulp Shredder to bring down a monster!*

CHAPTER 10

SECRET SEWERS OF SUPREME STINK

The Doom Raiders need the stinkiest goo in Skylands. Hold your nose and dive in to put a stop to their smelly supply!

Goals
- ◯ Shut down Krankcase's Goo Supply
- ◯ Prove you are a Skylander!

Dares
- ◯ No lives lost
- ◯ Find all 19 areas
- ◯ Defeat 135 enemies
- ◯ Defeat 2 Villains
- ◯ Open 2 *Traptanium* Gates

Difficult Dares
- ◯ Time to beat: 19:30
- ◯ Don't switch
- ◯ Complete 2 Villain Quests

Items
- ◯ 1 Story Scroll
- ◯ 4 Treasure Chests
- ◯ 2 Soul Gems
- ◯ 1 Winged Sapphire
- ◯ 1 Legendary Treasure
- ◯ 3 Hats

Areas
- ◯ Goober's Trail
- ◯ Outer Sewers Segue
- ◯ Flam Bam's Retreat
- ◯ Effluent Deck
- ◯ Grit Chamber-Tech
- ◯ Runoff Falls
- ◯ Backflow Alley
- ◯ The Storm Drain-Water
- ◯ Flow Drain Drop-off
- ◯ Spoiled Sanctum-Villains
- ◯ Drainage Vista
- ◯ Catwalk Cubby
- ◯ Drainage Central-Magic
- ◯ Inner Headworks-Fire
- ◯ Digestion Deck
- ◯ Going Down
- ◯ Splash Station
- ◯ Barge Basin
- ◯ Aqua Deck-Water

Outer Sewers Segue

It's worth seeing what you can sniff out in the sewer pipes, both above and below.

HINT: *After taking Flam Bam's Villain Quest, smash those* ***Traptanium*** *Crystals to unlock the Call of the Siren.*

EXTRA

Need to turn off the slime? Turn the giant cog in the direction of the arrows.

Grit Chamber

Solve the pulse puzzle to open the Flow Drain and then take a giant leap.

HINT: *In the Spoiled Sanctum, watch out for Goo Chompies. They turn into poisonous goo when bashed.*

Drainage Vista

It's another pulse puzzle. Line up the beams to blast the block. A super-jump pad lies beneath.

HINT: *Head through the Fire Elemental Gate for a Hat that you won't want to trash! You'll need to use a bounce pad or two.*

Digestion Deck

Wait for the goo sprayers to finish before racing across the platforms. You'll then be ready to take the plunge.

HINT: *Once out of the Deck, it's time for another sort of plunge—the kind that goes straight down!*

Splash Station

You'll need to connect the pipes using the shove blocks—but don't forget to connect both right and left sides.

HINT: *Once in Verl's arena, watch out for the Slime Eel. Its path is pure poison!*

CHAPTER 11

WILIKIN WORKSHOP

The Doom Raiders have taken over Kaos's old Wilikin factory. Well, they WOOD, wouldn't they? Do you see what I did there? Wood? Oh, suit yourself.

Goals

- ◯ Defeat Dr. Krankcase

Dares

- ◯ No lives lost
- ◯ Find all 19 areas
- ◯ Defeat 60 enemies
- ◯ Defeat 2 Villains
- ◯ Open 2 *Traptanium* Gates

Difficult Dares

- ◯ Time to beat: 16:30
- ◯ Don't switch
- ◯ Complete 3 Villain Quests

Items

- ◯ 1 Story Scroll
- ◯ 4 Treasure Chests
- ◯ 2 Soul Gems
- ◯ 1 Winged Sapphire
- ◯ 1 Legendary Treasure
- ◯ 2 Hats

Areas

- ◯ Wilikin Workers Town
- ◯ Wilikin Band Café
- ◯ Spool Storage Shack
- ◯ Wilikin Break Room
- ◯ Rail Car Repair Station
- ◯ Rail Car Repair Shop
- ◯ Toy Returns-Undead
- ◯ Rail Car Gauntlet-Fire
- ◯ Rail Car Arena
- ◯ Big Train Loading Area-Villains
- ◯ End of the Line
- ◯ Safe Toy Disposal-Magic
- ◯ Sneaky Pete's Saloon
- ◯ The Old Mill
- ◯ Rochester's House
- ◯ The Factory
- ◯ Smashing Area-Tech
- ◯ Crane Loading and Dropping
- ◯ Path to Dr. Krankcase

Wilikin Workers Town

Follow Kaos through the town, but don't forget to check out the houses as you pass. There's treasure and scrolls to be found.

HINT: *When walking the Rail Car Gauntlet, make use of the alcoves to ensure you don't get railroaded!*

Rail Car Arena

Scrap Shooter is waiting for you, so prepare for battle. Use the platform as a defense or to get a better angle.

HINT: *Make sure you've completed everything in the town. You'll be cut off after Scrap Shooter is trapped.*

Big Train Loading Area

It's worth exploring this sinister station. Jump down to find an Elemental Gate. Plus, you can put Scrap Shooter to work!

HINT: *If you need some health-giving food, pop over to the floating boat.*

Smashing Area

Once you're in the factory, follow the conveyor belts to the Smashing Area. Flick the switch at the end to get to the crane.

HINT: *Use the crane to drop bombs on the barriers. Who keeps bombs in a factory, anyway? Oh, that's right—Kaos!*

EXTRA

Watch out for the crates on the conveyor. They contain exploding mines!

Path to Dr. Krankcase

Prepare yourself for your biggest battle yet. Barrel-bots, goo, and revolving blades. The Doctor is in!

HINT: *When Krankcase attacks, look for the red target on the floor. That's where he's going to land.*

CHAPTER 12

TIME TOWN

Mags's Strange Anomaly Detector has uncovered that the Doom Raiders are trying to alter time itself. Stop them!

Goals

- ◯ Rescue Kaos from the Clocktower

Dares

- ◯ No lives lost
- ◯ Find all 19 areas
- ◯ Defeat 70 enemies
- ◯ Defeat 1 Villain
- ◯ Open 1 *Traptanium* Gate

Difficult Dares

- ◯ Time to beat: 11:50
- ◯ Don't switch
- ◯ Complete 2 Villain Quests

Items

- ◯ 1 Story Scroll
- ◯ 4 Treasure Chests
- ◯ 2 Soul Gems
- ◯ 1 Winged Sapphire
- ◯ 1 Legendary Treasure
- ◯ 2 Hats

Areas

- ◯ Grand Approach
- ◯ Father Cog's Patio
- ◯ Cog Family Fortune
- ◯ Pendulum Bob's House
- ◯ Moon Gear Rise
- ◯ Musical Terrace
- ◯ Chime Hammer Square–Air
- ◯ Wayward Cog Storage
- ◯ Main Spring Fly
- ◯ Backstage
- ◯ Sunny Side Narrows–Life
- ◯ Clockwork Innards
- ◯ Broken Toe Plateau–Earth
- ◯ Waterfall Cave
- ◯ Clockwork Courtyard–Villains
- ◯ Retired Clock Storage
- ◯ Cogsworth's Bed and Brunch
- ◯ Tower Approach–Air
- ◯ Owl Clock Gallery

Grand Approach

Push the gears into place to get the clockwork spinning, Portal Master.

HINT: *There's a Story Scroll to find on Moon Gear Rise. Hop around the cogs to find it.*

Chime Hammer Square

Da Pinchy is on hand to help you break the Steam Lock. Hit the pipes with the hammer. Timing is everything.

HINT: *Take a jump down before solving the Steam Lock Challenge. Someone needs a doctor!*

Main Spring Fly

After speaking to Florg, head up the conveyor belt and hit the button to get a Winged Sapphire!

HINT: *You might need to come back to this area after you've captured Cross Crow. Can you find out why?*

EXTRA

On Broken Toe Plateau, you'll need a pickaxe to climb the mountain.

Clockwork Courtyard

Take out the Villains to get to the next gear puzzle. Quick, time is running out.

HINT: *Jump on the moving platform, but head first to the steam lock to the right. There's a Villain to catch.*

Tower Approach

Once you can crow about your victory, it's back onto the platform and down to the last arena.

HINT: *Once inside the clock, hit the switches to line up the stairs.*

CHAPTER 13

THE FUTURE OF SKYLANDS

Da Pinchy is ready to take you ten thousand years into the future. Wolfgang awaits, Portal Master. Time to step up to the challenge.

Goals
- ◯ Enter the Big Bad Woofer
- ◯ Destroy the power conduits
- ◯ Defeat Wolfgang

Dares
- ◯ No lives lost
- ◯ Find all 13 areas
- ◯ Defeat 35 enemies
- ◯ Defeat 2 Villains
- ◯ Open 2 *Traptanium* Gates

Difficult Dares
- ◯ Time to beat: 12:40
- ◯ Don't switch
- ◯ Complete 2 Villain Quests

Items
- ◯ 1 Story Scroll
- ◯ 4 Treasure Chests
- ◯ 2 Soul Gems
- ◯ 1 Winged Sapphire
- ◯ 1 Legendary Treasure
- ◯ 3 Hats

Areas
- ◯ Arrival Platform
- ◯ Museum of Important Rockers-Light
- ◯ Ice Cream Planet-Earth
- ◯ Electro Bridge Controls
- ◯ Astro Bug Zapper
- ◯ Suborbital Combat Plaza-Enemies
- ◯ Containment Corner
- ◯ Mini Sun-Fire
- ◯ Antigrav Truck
- ◯ Space Dog Field-Tech
- ◯ Subatomic Particle Smasher
- ◯ Planet Ham
- ◯ Harmonic Hold
- ◯ Boss Fight Arena

Arrival Platform

After talking to Nort-Tron, jump down to find the Light Gate–if you can hear yourself think over Wolfgang's sound-check, of course!

HINT: *Flick the switch to deactivate the energy gates.*

Sub-Orbital Combat Plaza

Defeat the Villains to open the gate, but make sure you use the super-leap pad before joining the resistance.

HINT: *You'll have to take a trip in the Future-Cab in the future, once Wolfgang is safely trapped!*

EXTRA

Use your bridge-making skills in Containment Corner to jump over to that Legendary Treasure.

Anti-Grav Truck

Shove the blocks out of the way to line up your laser. Now blast the couplings so the grabbers release you!

HINT: *After a fight, follow Zeta Blobbers, flipping switches to let him pass energy barriers. There are safes to unlock along the way, too!*

Harmonic Hold

Zeta Blobbers will get you up to the Big Bad Woofer in his ship. You need to blast the power couplings to get into the concert.

HINT: *Take out the force fields and then turn the ship around before they can be raised again.*

Boss Fight Arena

It's Wolfgang's grand finale. Try to blast him when his guitar is stuck in the ground.

HINT: *When the laser show starts, watch the guiding lights to see where the beams will strike.*

CHAPTER 14

OPERATION: TROLL ROCKET STEAL

The Skylanders need a rocket to help save Skylands. Perhaps you can, ahem, borrow one from the trolls?

Goals

- ◯ Save the captive soldiers
- ◯ Break down the launch pad gate
- ◯ Confiscate the Rocket

Dares

- ◯ No lives lost
- ◯ Find all 17 areas
- ◯ Defeat 115 enemies
- ◯ Defeat 2 Villains
- ◯ Open 2 *Traptanium* Gates

Difficult Dares

- ◯ Time to beat: 11:15
- ◯ Don't switch
- ◯ Complete 2 Villain Quests

Items

- ◯ 1 Story Scroll
- ◯ 4 Treasure Chests
- ◯ 2 Soul Gems
- ◯ 1 Winged Sapphire
- ◯ 1 Legendary Treasure
- ◯ 4 Hats

Areas

- ◯ Mabu Main Base
- ◯ Crawler Canyon-Earth
- ◯ Mabu Base Entrance-Undead
- ◯ Southwest Tower
- ◯ Southeast Tower
- ◯ Battlements
- ◯ Troll Firing Range
- ◯ Tank Factory
- ◯ Factory Power Plant-Tech
- ◯ Factory Storage
- ◯ Troll Base Entrance-Undead
- ◯ Northwest Tower
- ◯ Northeast Tower
- ◯ Troll Main Base
- ◯ Troll Weapons Lab
- ◯ Mech Factory
- ◯ Mission Con-Troll

Crawler Canyon

Jump on the spiderlings' leaves to climb to the top of the termite hill. Just don't get knocked off on the way.

HINT: *You'll probably want to come back to this chapter later in the game, when you have a medic for the Mabu troops!*

Mabu Base Entrance

Defeat the trolls to free Nort, and then blow the barrier out of the way.

Hint: *Use the Health Regenifier to regain your strength.*

Battlements

Have the Mabu Defense Force Troops build you steps so you can reach the bomb. Then it's on to the Tank Factory.

HINT: *Step on the lit-up panels in the correct order to get the factory working again. You'll also need to pick up another bomb.*

EXTRA

Head back up the ramp by the bomb to gain entrance to Factory Storage. Cobra Cadabra will be glad you did!

Troll Main Base

Lead your army against the trolls. Keep an eye out for barriers to the left. Who knows who lies behind them?

HINT: *Follow the scorched path from the Troll Weapons Lab to find a Story Scroll and teleport pad.*

Mission Con-Troll

When fighting in Professor Nilbog's arena, watch out for the fire cannons opening. It's about to get hot, hot, hot!

HINT: *After Professor Nilbog transforms into Threatpack, keep an eye on the targets on the floor. You'll need to avoid his missiles.*

CHAPTER 15

SKYHIGHLANDS

The Sky Pirates have a gold detector. It's just what we need to find the Golden Queen. Take the battle to the skies, Portal Master.

Goals

- ◯ Take out the Sky Pirates
- ◯ Beat Hawkmongous to get the Prism

Dares

- ◯ No lives lost
- ◯ Find all 12 areas
- ◯ Defeat 50 enemies
- ◯ Defeat 1 Villain
- ◯ Open 2 *Traptanium* Gates

Difficult Dares

- ◯ Time to beat: 20:30
- ◯ Don't switch
- ◯ Complete 2 Villain Quests

Items

- ◯ 1 Story Scroll
- ◯ 4 Treasure Chests
- ◯ 1 Soul Gem
- ◯ 1 Winged Sapphire
- ◯ 1 Legendary Treasure
- ◯ 2 Hats

Areas

- ◯ Landing Platforms-Air
- ◯ Stolen Property Room
- ◯ Lower Defenses
- ◯ Lower Elevator
- ◯ Digger's Dungeon
- ◯ Middle Defenses-Water
- ◯ Upper Elevators
- ◯ Greenhouse-Life
- ◯ The Waterworks-Water
- ◯ Upper Defenses-Villains
- ◯ Lost and Found
- ◯ Cutting Platform

Landing Platforms

Grab the key from the Stolen Property Room and open the gate to a battle arena.

HINT: *You'll need to help your allies in the sky by manning the gun turrets. Try to hit the bonus gems, too!*

Stop off at Digger's Dungeon on the first gear platform for a Villain Quest!

Middle Defenses

Prepare for some air pirates to drop in. Watch where their chains fall. That's where they'll slide in to attack!

HINT: *When in a gun turret, hit the ships before they can turn and fire on you!*

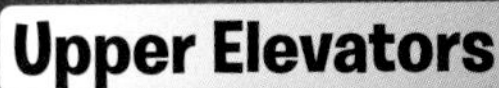

Upper Elevators

Jump down to the left from the first gear platform to grab a Soul Gem. You'll also want to pop into the Greenhouse.

HINT: *Getting to the Hatbox is a simple case of pushing the blocks into place. Tell all your friends.*

The Waterworks

Through this Elemental Gate, you'll need to hit the switches to raise the water levels.

HINT: *Don't fall into the water, or the works will drain dry again.*

Cutting Platform

The Prism is almost in your grasp. Take down Hawkmongous's band of Sky Pirates.

HINT: *Keep an eye on the Prism at all times. When all three stones are primed, it's about to fire!*

CHAPTER 16

THE GOLDEN DESERT

Mags's Strange Anomaly Detector has uncovered that the Doom Raiders are trying to alter time itself. Stop them!

Goals

- ◯ Clear out the Chompy Worms
- ◯ Save Cali from the Golden Queen

Dares

- ◯ No lives lost
- ◯ Find all 10 areas
- ◯ Defeat 55 enemies
- ◯ Defeat 2 Villains
- ◯ Open 2 *Traptanium* Gates

Difficult Dares

- ◯ Time to beat: 15:50
- ◯ Don't switch
- ◯ Complete 2 Villain Questss

Items

- ◯ 1 Story Scroll
- ◯ 4 Treasure Chests
- ◯ 1 Soul Gem
- ◯ 1 Winged Sapphire
- ◯ 1 Legendary Treasure
- ◯ 2 Hats

Areas

- ◯ X's Shifting Sands-Earth
- ◯ The Dust Bowl
- ◯ The Temple of Topaz
- ◯ The Howling Caverns-Villain
- ◯ Hole in the Wall
- ◯ The Golden Springs
- ◯ The Earthen Alcove-Earth
- ◯ The Windy Watch-Air
- ◯ The Windy Heights
- ◯ The Jeweled Coliseum

X's Shifting Sands

You'll have your hands full fighting enemies, but watch out for Villain Quests, too!

HINT: *Destroy the tombs in the battle arenas to stop more enemies from popping up!*

The Dust Bowl

Cover Cali by shooting the Chompy Worms using the catapult.

HINT: *When the Worms burrow, destroy anything they can use as a shield!*

The Temple of Topaz

Push the blocks into holes to get to the switches. Once everything's in place, the tongue bridge will stick out. How rude!

HINT: *Once in the Howling Caverns, try to grab falling bombs. You'll need to throw one back!*

The Golden Springs

Solve the pulse puzzle to access the stairs, then return to the Howling Caverns past the spikes.

HINT: *Head down once you're in the Golden Springs if you want to find an Elemental Gate.*

EXTRA

Solve the Lockmaster Imp's puzzle to find a treasure chest.

The Jeweled Coliseum

The Golden Queen has her Undead arena waiting for you. Three waves of terror–and all with an audience, too!

HINT: *Catch the bombs and throw them at the three columns to bring the house down.*

CHAPTER 17

LAIR OF THE GOLDEN QUEEN

The Golden Queen is turning everything in Skylands to gold, and is planning to use the Ultimate Weapon to attack Skylanders Academy. Take the fight to her, Portal Master!

Goals
- ◯ Find and defeat the Golden Queen

Dares
- ◯ No lives lost
- ◯ Find all 10 areas
- ◯ Defeat 55 enemies
- ◯ Defeat 2 Villains
- ◯ Open 2 *Traptanium* Gates

Difficult Dares
- ◯ Time to beat: 13:40
- ◯ Don't switch
- ◯ Complete 2 Villain Quests

Items
- ◯ 1 Story Scroll
- ◯ 4 Treasure Chests
- ◯ 1 Soul Gem
- ◯ 1 Winged Sapphire
- ◯ 1 Legendary Treasure
- ◯ 3 Hats

Areas
- ◯ Tomb of the Forgotten Queen
- ◯ The Halls of Treachery-Fire
- ◯ Cradle of the Four Winds-Air
- ◯ The Secret Vault
- ◯ The Darkest Reach-Villains
- ◯ The Parade of Broken Soldiers-Undead
- ◯ The Seat of Flowing Gold
- ◯ The Evershifting Abyss-Magic
- ◯ Heart of Gold
- ◯ The Temple of the Divine Treasure

Tomb of the Forgotten Queen

Open the doors by lining up the power beams. First shove the blocks out of the way so the beams aren't, you know, blocked.

HINT: *Use the lever to swivel the crystals to complete the energy lock. The doors will open before you can say, um, "open"!*

EXTRA

Jump into the swirling mist, if you dare! Terror and treasure await!

The Halls of Treachery

Those bridges aren't safe. Stay too long on the cracked tiles and you'll fall.

HINT: *Stones with a green cross on them can heal you–just watch out for the spears!*

The Parade of Broken Soldiers

Don't get caught by the Golden Queen's spy guys. Jump into the safe areas as they sweep by.

HINT: *You might also try burying the spies in the skies beneath the odd pillar or two.*

The Seat of Flowing Gold

You'll have to take down Bad Juju plus beat Nut at Skystones Smash to get to this chilling chamber!

HINT: *Have I mentioned that stones with glowing runes will hurt you? No? Then I hope you haven't been stepping on them!*

The Temple of the Divine Treasure

It's the fight of your life! You'll never hit the Golden Queen while she's in her force field. Wait until she's vulnerable.

HINT: *Knock the rubble out of the way when the Queen is on your tail. Oh, and run. Run very, very fast.*

CHAPTER 18

THE ULTIMATE WEAPON

Kaos has betrayed us and now is after the one person who continues to foil his despicable plans. Not even Earth is safe from his power! Stop him before he stops you!

Goals

- ◯ Reach the top of the Great Machine
- ◯ Defeat Kaos!

Dares

- ◯ No lives lost
- ◯ Find all 11 areas
- ◯ Defeat 40 enemies
- ◯ Defeat 2 Villains
- ◯ Open 2 *Traptanium* Gates

Difficult Dares

- ◯ Time to beat: 29:55
- ◯ Don't switch
- ◯ Complete 2 Villain Quests

Items

- ◯ 1 Story Scroll
- ◯ 4 Treasure Chests
- ◯ 1 Soul Gem
- ◯ 1 Winged Sapphire
- ◯ 1 Legendary Treasure
- ◯ 2 Hats

Areas

- ◯ Loading Zone
- ◯ Receiving Dock
- ◯ Power Re-router-Dark
- ◯ Relay System
- ◯ Matter Refactoring Room-Air
- ◯ Repair Platform H-Villains
- ◯ The Balloon Return-Tech
- ◯ External Power Sorter
- ◯ Power Exhaust Ports-Fire
- ◯ The Grinder
- ◯ The Flywheels-Villains
- ◯ Final Battle Arena

Relay System

Line up the pulse puzzles to open the doors to the Ultimate Weapon's inner workings. You know the drill.

HINT: *Another pulse puzzle lies ahead in the Matter Refactoring Room. Wait for the pulse to pass and then switch!*

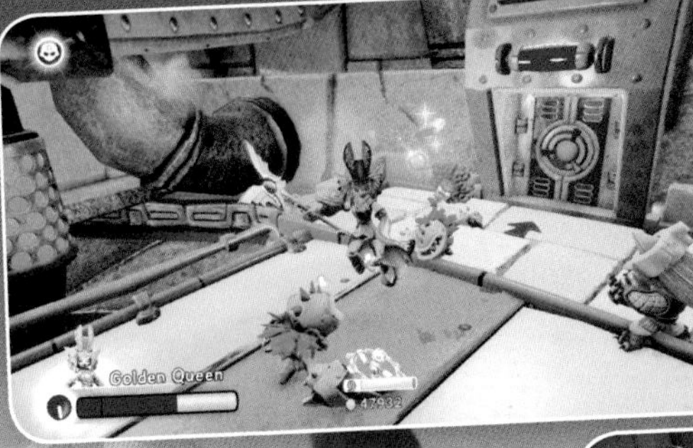

Repair Platform H

Looks like Kaos got the drop on you. Activate the goo pod to blow your way through the gate. You'll need to defeat all the minions to continue.

HINT: *Head right for a lighter-than-air challenge and a final word from Flynn! He does go on, doesn't he?*

External Power Sorter

Avoid the serpents' breath as you climb to the higher level.

HINT: *You'll have to come back this way once Smoke Scream is happily in a trap. Okay, so he probably won't be that happy!*

EXTRA

Need an extra boost before the final battle? Persephone is on hand for a last-minute upgrade!

Power Exhaust Ports

Trap Smoke Scream and then defeat the minions to gain access to the Exhaust Ports.

HINT: *Watch out for energy discharges as you leap up to the Grinder. More pulse puzzles are ahead. Literally!*

Final Battle Arena

Okay, so the last final battle wasn't the final battle at all! Avoid Kaos's energy rings and *Traptanium* swords!

HINT: *Use the correct Villains to counteract Kaos's elemental bullets, but be warned—the fiend can heal himself!*

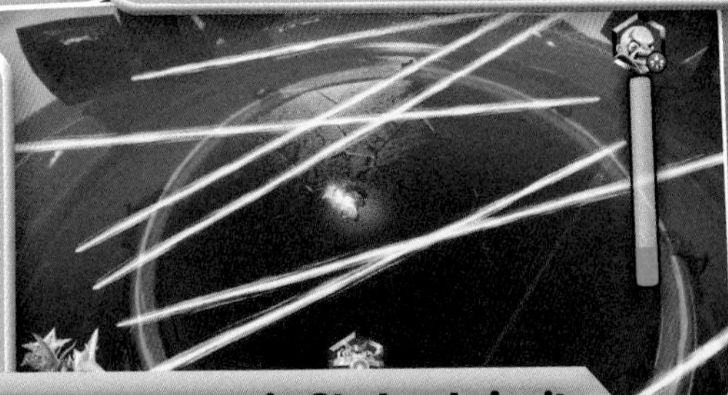

Your adventure in Skylands isn't over yet. Turn the page to discover whole new worlds to explore!

ADVENTURE PACKS

Nightmare Express

Flynn went out to search for the Trolly Grail, but now he's gotten into some trouble. Hop onto the Nightmare Express to help chase a thieving Cyclops, and watch out for bombs!

Goals
- ◯ Find the artifact in the temple
- ◯ Take down the Troll Mega Tank
- ◯ Retake the Trolly Grail

Dares
- ◯ No lives lost
- ◯ Find all 24 areas
- ◯ Defeat 70 enemies
- ◯ Defeat 2 Villains
- ◯ Open 2 *Traptanium* Gates

Difficult Dares
- ◯ Time to beat: 11:50
- ◯ Don't switch
- ◯ Complete 2 Villain Quests

Items
- ◯ 1 Story Scroll
- ◯ 4 Treasure Chests
- ◯ 1 Winged Sapphire
- ◯ 1 Legendary Treasure
- ◯ 4 Hats

Mirror of Mystery

In this mirrored universe, the good guys are the bad guys, and Kaos and the trolls are on your side. What a wacky world!

Goals

- ◯ Construct a Troll Mech
- ◯ Destroy Persephone's Tree
- ◯ Defeat Evilon

Dares

- ◯ No lives lost
- ◯ Find all 18 areas
- ◯ Defeat 45 enemies
- ◯ Defeat 2 Villains
- ◯ Open 2 *Traptanium* Gates

Difficult Dares

- ◯ Time to beat: 8:55
- ◯ Don't switch
- ◯ Complete 2 Villain Quests

Items

- ◯ 1 Story Scroll
- ◯ 4 Treasure Chests
- ◯ 1 Winged Sapphire
- ◯ 1 Legendary Treasure
- ◯ 3 Hats

Goals

- ◯ Reclaim the Dark Eye of Tomorrow

Dares

- ◯ No lives lost
- ◯ Find all 17 areas
- ◯ Defeat 50 enemies
- ◯ Defeat 1 Villain
- ◯ Open 2 *Traptanium* Gates

Difficult Dares

- ◯ Time to beat: 10:15
- ◯ Don't switch
- ◯ Complete 1 Villain Quest

Items

- ◯ 1 Story Scroll
- ◯ 4 Treasure Chests
- ◯ 1 Soul Gem
- ◯ 1 Winged Sapphire
- ◯ 1 Legendary Treasure
- ◯ 3 Hats

Midnight Museum

The Villain Nightshade is trying to steal the Dark Eye of Unvisibility! To catch this dastardly thief, you'll have to act like a thief and break into the heavily guarded Midnight Museum.

Sunscraper Spire

This part of Skylands used to be cut off from the rest of the universe, but now there is a strange energy circling the towers. Find out what's going on—but be careful! The Light element is still mysterious to us.

Goals

- ◯ Direct the beams into the crystal
- ◯ Defeat Luminous in the tower

Dares

- ◯ No lives lost
- ◯ Find all 18 areas
- ◯ Defeat 90 enemies
- ◯ Defeat 1 Villain
- ◯ Open 2 *Traptanium* Gates

Difficult Dares

- ◯ Time to beat: 12:50
- ◯ Don't switch
- ◯ Complete 1 Villain Quest

Items

- ◯ 1 Story Scroll
- ◯ 4 Treasure Chests
- ◯ 1 Soul Gem
- ◯ 1 Winged Sapphire
- ◯ 1 Legendary Treasure
- ◯ 3 Hats

AFTER THE ADVENTURE

RUMBLE CLUB

Brock's back with brand-new arena challenges!

Phoenix Nest

1. Artillery Attack

Avoid the falling bombs as you fight.

HINT: *Watch out for those Phoenix chicks!*

2. Nest Ball

Grab the superball to become big and strong.

HINT: *Don't get hit. You'll lose the ball!*

3. Birdy Bombs

Look out! When an enemy is defeated, they drop an explosive mine.

HINT: *Use the Phoenix chicks as shields during attacks.*

4. Perilous Perch Skirmish

Bombs, superballs, and mines in one Arena!

HINT: *Don't let your enemies grab that superball!*

Dreamquake

1. Monster Multiplier

Stop your enemies from getting into the magic circles. They'll clone themselves.

HINT: *Why not stand in the circles yourself?*

2. Flag, You're It!

Raise a flag and send a shockwave rushing out toward your enemies.

HINT: *Don't let the minions raise their own flags!*

3. Counting Sheep

Protect your sheep from marauding minions.

HINT: *Use a Skylander with a long range to shoot from a safe distance.*

4. Bad Dream Brawl

The game changes with every stage. First superball, then flags and, finally, clones.

HINT: *Defend one flag at a time!*

Drain of Sorrows

1. Germ Wars

The minions are sick. Don't let them infect you!

HINT: *Brock will throw you helpful medicine.*

2. Sheep Flush

The sheep are back. Protect the flock.

HINT: *If your Skylander can take the punishment, stand beneath the enemies' entrance.*

3. Sewer-Ball

It's superball but with added cloning.

HINT: *Use the Slime Eel's trail as a defense.*

4. Slime Time Tournament

Sick enemies who explode? Superball with flags? Good grief!

HINT: *Worry about the flags and then go for the ball!*

Exhaust Junction

1. You're MINE

Mined enemies are trying to clone themselves! Stop them!

HINT: *Watch out for those exhaust cannons!*

2. Artillery 2: With a Vengeance

Avoid the pirate bombs while fighting enemies!

HINT: *Can you use the high ground of the arena?*

3. Don't Get Hit

A single hit will end your arena challenge!

HINT: *Grab Brock's shield power-ups.*

4. Flaming Flag Finale

Try to control as many flags as you can while facing changing challenges!

HINT: *Make sure to always have at least one flag raised.*

Quicksand Coliseum

1. Mighty Ball Bombardment

Superball causes even more damage when you add pirate bombs!

HINT: *Avoid the statue's eye lasers!*

2. Multiplication Fever

Sick fighters are trying to clone themselves again!

HINT: *There's a Chompy Worm in the sand! Gulp!*

3. Flames and Flags Forever

It's hard to defend your flags when Brock's firing at you all the time!

HINT: *The lasers will follow you. Lead them to your foes!*

4. Scorched Sand Showdown

Enemies really like mines! But also changing challenges!

HINT: *Use ranged attacks to help you avoid the mines.*

There's a new arena to purchase in Auric's store!

Brock's Rumble Clubhouse

1. The Flame Game

Brock loves fire! Watch for fire blasters!

HINT: *Steer clear of the arena's edges.*

2. Combusti-Ball

It's like pinball but with cannons! What's not to like?

HINT: *Let your trapped Villain take some of the hits.*

3. Laser Invader

Lasers everywhere! Jump over them or run away.

HINT: *Choose a Skylander with a good ranged attack.*

4. A Fight to Remember

Anything goes! Brock's pulling out all the stops for this one!

HINT: *React quickly to changing challenges.*

KAOS DOOM CHALLENGE

If it isn't enough that Kaos is determined to conquer Skylands, now he's gone and cursed the Academy's challenge zone! Never fear, Portal Master, here are Cali's tips on how to beat his challenges of ultimate doom!

1. Your task is simple. Stop the minions from reaching Kaos's Mysterious Box of Doom.
2. In between waves of enemies, build defensive towers to help you hold back the tide.
3. When your towers are built and you're ready to face another wave, activate the handily titled wave switch.
4. Enemies will attack your towers in an attempt to bring them down. Protect them rather than the Mysterious Box of Doom.
5. Standing next to your towers helps them regenerate.
6. Keep a lookout for food to give you a boost during battles.
7. After wave three you'll need Skylanders of specific elements to build towers. Good luck, Portal Master!

A little treat for Kaos fans is hidden in the game's end credits!

HIDDEN ACHIEVEMENTS AND TROPHIES

Every time you complete a chapter, you'll receive an Achievement or a Trophy, depending on your console. Not all consoles award Achievements and Trophies. Here's a handy list to help you track them down . . .

Achievement	Requirement
Statue Smasher	Destroy 4 stone Chompy heads in Chompy Mountain
Preemptive Power	Destroy 1 Dropship in The Phoenix Psanctuary
Cannon Completest	Destroy 8 Troll Transports during the flying sequence in Chef Zeppelin
Pipe Down	Destroy 4 stacks of pipes using the crane on Dredger's Yacht in Rainfish Riviera
No Coins Left Behind	Collect 20 coins while following Marsha through the mist in Monster Marsh
Ball Sprawler	Knock 12 Golden Balls off the waterfall in the Meditative Pool area in Telescope Towers
Evilikin Eliminator	Shoot 20 Evilikin Runners during the flying sequence in Mystic Mill
No Goo For You!	Travel to Splash Station without taking any damage from goo in Secret Sewers of Supreme Stink
Ride the Rails	Ride the train to the end of the line in Wilikin Workshop
Da Pinchy Defacer	Destroy 5 Da Pinchy statues in Time Town
Just to be Safe	Take down every shield unit during the flying sequence in The Future of Skylands
Exhaust All Possibilities	Complete the arena battle without getting hit by rocket exhaust in Operation: Troll Rocket Steal
Look, Ma, No Rockets!	Shoot down 30 Sky Pirates without using rockets in Skyhighlands
Garden Gladiator	Destroy 10 cacti in The Golden Desert.
High-wire Act	Complete all the tile floor puzzles without falling in Lair of the Golden Queen
Do a Barrel Roll	Collect 9 coins while falling down the Machine Heart in The Ultimate Weapon
Savior of Skylands IV	Complete Story Mode on any difficulty setting
Dream a Little Nightmare	Complete Story Mode on the Nightmare difficulty setting
Kaos Mode Master	Defeat 100 enemies in Kaos Mode
Star Star	Earn 50 Stars in Kaos Mode
Arena Mogul	Unlock Brock's special arena
Chairman of the Rumble Club	Complete all Arena levels
Not Out of Your Element	Unlock your first Elemental area
Hero Hunter	Capture 10 Villains
Skystones Scavenger	Collect 20 Skystones
All the Way Up!	Level up any Skylander to level 20
Wow, That's Tough!	Achieve Portal Master Rank 5
Road to Redemption	Complete a captured Villain's Quest

Note: not all consoles award Achievements and Trophies.